Treadwell Walden

The Great Meaning of Metanoia

An Underdeveloped Chapter in the Life and Teaching of Christ

Treadwell Walden

The Great Meaning of Metanoia
An Underdeveloped Chapter in the Life and Teaching of Christ

ISBN/EAN: 9783337027988

Printed in Europe, USA, Canada, Australia, Japan

Cover: Foto ©Lupo / pixelio.de

More available books at **www.hansebooks.com**

THE GREAT MEANING OF METANOIA

AN UNDEVELOPED CHAPTER IN THE LIFE AND TEACHING OF CHRIST

A NEW EDITION
WITH A SUPPLEMENTARY ESSAY

BY
TREADWELL WALDEN

NEW-YORK
THOMAS WHITTAKER
1896

INSCRIBED
WITH DEVOTED LOVE
TO

MY WIFE,
GRACE GORDON WALDEN.

"233 CLARENDON STREET,
"BOSTON, October 15, 1881.

"DEAR WALDEN: I have just read your 'Metánoia' through from beginning to end, and I want to tell you how much I enjoyed it, and how much I thank you for sending it to me.

"It is full of inspiration.

" It makes one think of Christian faith as positive and constructive, and not merely destructive and remedial.

"It makes the work of Christ seem worthy of Christ.

"I thank you truly, both for writing it and for giving it to me.

"Your sincere friend,
"PHILLIPS BROOKS."

PREFACE.

THE first of these Essays appeared in the "American Church Review" for July, 1881—following the memorable day in May when the Revised Version of the New Testament was issued. The paper was soon afterwards reprinted separately, and in 1882 was put into book form by the present publisher.

Although its point was made timely by the revision, and by the astonishing fact that, in a work expressly undertaken in this age to correct the misapprehensions of a former age, a mistranslation involving such consequences had been overpassed and perpetuated, yet the Essay did not set out to be a criticism of the New Version in this particular. It could not help falling into something like it, but its main purpose was to draw attention to, and to be a popular exposition of, a word in whose enormous potentiality of meaning lay, as I believed, a more true and more catholic, a more spiritual and more philo-

Preface.

sophical, interpretation of Christianity. The Essay could have done as well for this—with a little modification—if the revisers had adopted a new rendering which was, in any degree, sympathetic with the real import of the original.

As such, I am glad to say—after the novelty of the New Version had passed—the Essay seems to have been accepted: simply as an exposition in itself, that might at any time be in order; and as a contribution, called for under the circumstances, to the knowledge and the spirit which ought to inspire that comprehensive English expression or that happy combination of words—varying according to their connection in the text—which may venture sometime hence to represent the idea of Μετάνοια; a word of whose fullness, in its initial position, the New Testament itself can be the only adequate translation, for, in that initial position, it is the key-note of its whole strain.

There was nothing new in the view itself. If there had been, it could not have been true. It was as old as the apostolic age. And the revival of it was only an attempt to uncover and clear out a partially choked well.

Preface.

The Greek expression lay directly under the eye of any reader of the original, manifestly opening down to a great depth, provided his eye was disengaged enough from prepossessions to be alive to the fact. The word bore the hint of what it was on its very face: an intimation that the whole inward nature of man was appealed to, all its springs of action, all its possibilities of affection. Every scholar was aware of its literal meaning—and that meaning alone was in itself enough to suggest the dropping of an exploring plummet. Why this was not done, why what was so obvious was overlooked, perhaps the second Essay may explain.

Neither was there anything new in the endeavor to recover the lost meaning of the word. There had been, even so far back as the remote age in which its present customary curb and covering had first been imposed upon it, an instinctive misgiving that its full depth had not been sounded. But the misgiving had been overborne because it was not pronounced enough. The Reformation, also, developed a restiveness under the same ancient limitation—for mud, as well as water, was being drawn up now—but the restiveness wrought no real purification, because it was not articulate enough. At a later day—that is, a hundred years ago—an orthodox but independent Scotchman, Dr. George Campbell, exposed the whole imposition with startling distinctness, and succeeded so well in sweeping the fabric away that many since his day—several recent translators among them—owe all their new conception of the truth to him. But in both his and their contentment with the substitute "reformation" for "*repentance*" there lay an implication of externalism, which betrayed, apparently, a lack of insight into the spiritual profundity of the original expression. The new rendering did not, also, popularly prevail, though pointing to the practical result in the life, because the old one, though falling short of the whole truth ("regeneration"), did at last reach down far enough to stir the oft-stagnant pool of the conscience and the heart.

It has turned out that the absolute insight into the meaning of the word has in our own day been given to two scholars like De Quincey and Matthew Arnold, and has found its first distinct expression through them, because, unlike all that have gone before them, their vision was unhampered by any theological preconception, and by the necessity of looking for an available form of English translation. It was simply this which left their powers of perception clear; both open-eyed to a palpable meaning, and free-handed in their statement of it. But they did not raise a signal-flag over the fact when they found it, as if it were a discovery, nor concern themselves especially in identifying the word with its issues. They took its evident idea as a matter of course, recognized it as the original spring-head of the Gospel, restored it to its natural condition, and passed on. Hence their brief and casual allusions to it have escaped the attention that was their due.

I was far on in the preparation of the first Essay before I ran accidentally upon the passage in De Quincey, and well on in the second before I came as accidentally upon the coincidence with it and yet variation from it of Matthew Arnold—the one indicating the intellectual sweep, the other the ethical depth of the word; but I have been glad indeed to owe to them both an encouraging and illumining inspiration in the endeavor to show that the principle enunciated by "Metanoia" in the outset of the Gospel was profound enough to be the underlying and prevailing idea of the New Testament from beginning to end, and to suggest the application of its interpretative potency to the teaching of Christ and His apostles. And this—the most obvious thing in the world to do when once on the track of it—is all that appears to be new.

But even this could be only generally and superficially intimated in a review article. Still, such as it was, the idea was a surprise and even a revelation to many people. And there have been indications enough that it has since taken a wide hold. I do not receive this impression only from the many earnest letters and other like evidences which have come to me, or from an occasional reference in a recent commentary or expository paper, but from the fact that the view seems to have entered largely into pulpit teaching and current thought. It has been made the theme of many sermons, and it has given occasion to a number of printed essays and magazine articles, several even of a philosophical character. The word "Metanoia" itself has also become quite a familiar English expression, not only for what it really means, but, I fear, in some cases where an ignorant enthusiasm has laid hold of it, for what it cannot be understood to mean.

It has been made the ground, however, of one interesting suggestion, by a writer in the "Popular Science Monthly," who has copiously quoted the Essay, that the term "Metagnostic"—or, better, the words "Metanostic" and "Metanoëtic"—should displace the idea conveyed by "Agnostic," as expressing positively, affirmatively, and hopefully, instead of negatively and despairingly, the attitude even of the purely scientific mind in the presence of the Unknown. The suggestion, it seems, failed with Mr. Huxley, when presented to him, because a slight inaccuracy in the statement of the primary force of the proposed words gave him an opportunity to evade it; but the idea has, however, gone far enough into usage to bring about the introduction of "Metagnostic," with this signification, in the "Century Dictionary."

It is all this and the like of it that has kept the memory of the Essay afloat these

Preface.

fourteen years and more, that has caused a continual inquiry for it, and that has now led to its reissue, after being long out of print.

In publishing it again I ought to say that I have gone over the whole ground with much thorough and painstaking study, and have verified all its positions so satisfactorily that I have seen no reason to change any of them. Indeed, so largely and variously has the subject opened and enriched itself, both in its Scriptural illustration and its practical application, that the present little volume seems to stand yet only on the threshold of the whole contemplation. But I have been under an exigency of brevity in bringing it out, and can only hope that it may serve its purpose as an introduction, if no more.

The book has fallen into a threefold form: first, the original Essay, slightly retouched and with a few notes added; second, a Supplementary Essay, mainly to supply a strong point of view in which the other was necessarily lacking, but incidentally including such further intimations of the bearing of "Metanoia" as could be thrown out by the way; and third, a group of selected comments upon the subject by different distinguished hands —five of them revisers—to show that I do not stand alone in my estimate of its necessity and importance.

The last in the list of these—by no means the least—is Phillips Brooks. I have also set the whole of the opening part of his note to me in the forefront of this new edition, partly under an impulse of personal affection, partly because of the comprehensiveness and force of what he wrote. He was my cherished friend for thirty years, a pride and delight to me as I saw him advancing in the strength of the breadth and depth of the truth he proclaimed, and under the blessing which attended a pure, a noble, and a devoted life. In these few words, out of his very heart, he seized with characteristic insight the vital point of the whole consideration, and they are of that very quality in thought, conviction, and expression which was the secret of his power both as a preacher and as a man. In the midst of the concentric circles drawn round the mark, as it was also recognized by the others that I have quoted, he thus laid his finger upon the central white:—

"It makes one think of Christian faith as positive and constructive, and not merely destructive and remedial.

"It makes the work of Christ seem worthy of Christ."

In *that* he said *all*.

T. W.

CAMBRIDGE, MASS.,
December, 1895.

CONTENTS.

ESSAY I.

THE GREAT MEANING OF THE WORD METÁNOIA: LOST IN THE OLD VERSION, UNRECOVERED IN THE NEW.

CHAPTER		PAGE
I.	The New Testament Idea of Metánoia...	1
II.	"Metánoia" Mistranslated "*Repentance*"	13
III.	The Intellectual as well as Moral Compass of Metánoia	31
IV.	The Inaugural Action of Metánoia in the First Age...	45
V.	Metanoia the Method of Christ's Teaching	60
VI.	The Metanoia of St. Paul—Faith and Renewal	71
VII.	Metanoia the Word of Christ to the Present Age	83
	NOTE.—The View of Matthew Arnold	91

Contents.

ESSAY II.

THE ECLIPSE OF METÁNOIA BY PŒNITENTIA.

CHAPTER	PAGE
I. An Impossible Expedient to End it: "*Repentance*" to be Made to Mean Metanoia	95
II. Μετάνοια Transfigured Greek	100
III. "*Repentance*" Persistent Latin	108
IV. The Roman Utilization of "*Repentance*"	117
V. The Gospel in the Shadow of the Law	123
VI. "Disastrous Twilight" in the Revised Version	130
VII. The Power of Latin Prescription	139
VIII. The True Interpretation	145

ASSENTING WITNESSES.

A Word Introductory 152
The Comments of:
I. The Right Rev. Brooke Foss Westcott, D.D., D.C.L. 153
II. The Rev. Professor Alexander Roberts, D.D. 154
III. The Rev. Howard Crosby, D.D., LL.D. 155

Contents.

LETTER		PAGE
IV.	The Rev. Philip Schaff, D.D., LL.D	156
V.	The Very Rev. E. H. Plumptre, D.D.	156
VI.	The Rev. Edward White	157
VII.	The Rev. Professor Alexander V. G. Allen, D.D.	158
VIII.	The Rev. Professor J. F. Garrison, D.D.	160
IX.	The Rev. Elisha Mulford, LL.D	163
X.	The Rev. Edward T. Bartlett, D.D.	163
XI.	The Rev. Benjamin Franklin, D.D.	165
XII.	The Right Rev. Phillips Brooks, D.D.	166

I AM COME A LIGHT INTO THE WORLD, THAT WHOSOEVER BELIEVETH ON ME MAY NOT ABIDE IN THE DARKNESS.
John xii. 46.

THE GREAT MEANING OF THE WORD METÁNOIA: LOST IN THE OLD VERSION, UNRECOVERED IN THE NEW.

I.

THE NEW TESTAMENT IDEA OF METÁNOIA.

METÁNOIA is the Greek word—and letter for letter an English one, if we desire it —which bears the sublime burden of the original proclamation of the gospel.

It represents the first utterance of John the Baptist as the herald of the Christ, and the first utterance of Jesus the Christ as the herald of the kingdom of God. It was their summons to mankind, preceding the announcement of the power that was approaching, of the revelation that was at hand.

If we recur to the image involved in the words "herald," "proclamation"—the image implied in the narrative—it was the note of a trumpet outside the walls, and the call of a messenger to open the gates.

In order the better to get at its meaning, let us now imagine some one who has never read the English New Testament, and who has had no especial bias given to his ideas by any theological system. All we will suppose for him is a knowledge of Greek and a spiritual instinct which will enable him to rise into the frequent transcendental meaning of the Greek of the New Testament.

He knows enough to know that he is dealing with the record of a divine revolution in the affairs of men, and that the human language to which the account was committed is struggling to utter adequately the depth of inspiration behind it.

He knows that the record was committed to writing only after the bearings of the history were fully understood and the conception of its meaning was fully matured.

He knows that what is before him is a condensation as to events, and a translation as to ideas; in other words, if we confine the remark to the four gospels, that the historical part is as brief as it is profound, and that the doctrinal part is not only briefly and profoundly expressed, but was transferred to the Greek from the Aramaic vernacular in which it was at first expansively spoken.

He is prepared, therefore, to see not only a representative depth in each event, but, especially, a comprehensive force in every cardinal word.

In the very outset of the life of Christ he comes upon the word "Metánoia," and in a connection which gives it the all-prominent place. He takes in the significance of its position at once. It conveys the summons of the herald, and of the herald who was freighted with the good news which the whole New Testament afterwards unfolds. Here in epitome, he naturally thinks, must be all the "Upward Calling" of God. No word, therefore, in the New Testament can be greater than this.

Hence he must interpret it as a condensed expression of what was originally said in large, and as an expression, also, which was fixed upon long after the event, when everything was understood, as the fit one to carry the great burden. If this is its anticipatory reach, if this is its heralding grasp, he naturally sets about inquiring what is its history and what its elementary weight.

When we imagine such a fresh reader of the Greek Testament as this we place ourselves in the situation to pursue his inquiry.

The literal meaning of "Metánoia," or, rather, the nearest expression to it in English, is "Change of Mind," a phrase too much worn by familiar use to be available as a rendering, but an idea capable of many equivalent variations in the English tongue. It will be more convenient, however, for our present purpose to employ the phrase as if its native force had not been thus impaired.

What word is more expressive than "Change"? what more comprehensive than "Mind"?

"Change," in the radical sense we here intend, when applied to the "mind," ought to suggest something hardly short of a transmutation; not of essence, of course, but of consciousness. We understand by a change of place the occupation of another place; a change of condition, another condition; a change of form, another form. We can imagine the otherwise unchangeable man undergoing, in like manner, a "Change of Mind"; what Coleridge coined the word "transmentation" to express: a sort of mental transfiguration, under which the Mind, when placed in a new situation, thinks new thoughts, receives new impressions, forms new tastes, inclinations, purposes, develops new aptitudes; such a Change may be good or evil, but such a change is possible.

For what is the "Mind"? It is that spiritual part of us which receives and assimilates whatever it has an affinity for in the world outside, whether that world be spiritual or material. It is the whole group of faculties which compose the intelligence. It is sight and perception, thought and reflection, apprehension and comprehension—all that is popularly known as the intellect or understanding. But it also embraces more than this, namely, a large portion of the moral and affectional nature. It occupies the realm of the heart. Thus it comes about that, in common speech, the terms "mind" and "heart" are often interblended, one overlapping the field of the other. We speak of the heart as if it were the thinking principle. It has its thoughts as well as its affections. We also speak of the mind as if it had feelings as well as perceptions. The will, too, seems to be as much at home in one as in the other. What the mind fancies it will do, it shortly resolves to do, is minded to do. What the mind also fastens its attention upon, it shortly fastens its love upon. We love with the whole mind as well as with the whole heart, soul, and strength.

When, therefore, we speak of the Mind, we often mean the heart as well as the brain, but we never mean the heart without the brain. The Mind proper is the masculine, intellectual element, strong and foremost, of which the heart is the feminine, affectional counterpart, always in attendance upon it, always at one with it. As "Man" is the generic name for Adam and Eve, so "Mind" is the generic name for this twofold nature of man.[1]

When, then, "Mind" means so much, and "Change" may be made to mean so much,

[1] It may be well to remember that "man" and "mind" are etymologically the same. A change of the Mind, therefore, is a change of the Man.

to speak of a "Change of Mind" is to stand on the verge of a great conception.

Now we are introduced into the fullness of the Greek word "Metánoia." *Noūs* is the precise equivalent of "Mind." It is intellect, first and foremost, but it is intellect interblended, in its action, with the nature behind it. There is no mystic partition dividing the one from the other. It is the whole soul. It is Mind, first, in the sense of perception, knowledge, thought. It is Mind, next, in the sense of feeling, disposition, will. And *Noūs* is the body of the word "Metánoia." *Metá* is a preposition which, when compounded with *Noūs*, means *after*.[1] Metánoia is the After-Mind: perception, knowledge, thought, feeling, disposition, will, *afterwards*. The Mind has entered upon a new stage, upon something beyond. If the prefix were *pró*, "Prónoia" would mean perception before, thought before, a state of mind before experience. But Metánoia is a state of mind after experi-

---

[1] "*After*," in such a connection, denotes the idea of *change* or *transformation*. Νοέω, to *see*, to *perceive*. Μετανοέω, to *see* or *perceive afterwards*. Hence, to *change one's view*.

The Great Meaning of Metánoia.

ence; the mental condition which has developed itself after an entirely new set of circumstances has encompassed and invaded the consciousness.

Metá, therefore, introduces the Mind in the act of progress, a "change" taking place either by evolution or by revolution; development through any cause or in any form, when the Mind is operated upon by considerations within or by conditions without.[1]

In this statement of the capacity of the

---

[1] A lay friend, after this paper was written, sent us the following: "The force of *Metá* is clearly this, viz., 'end for end,' or 'in the opposite direction,' or 'anew.' . . . For the root of *Metá* is the English 'mid,' and *Metá* is at bottom the English 'amid.' From this idea (one of situation) it progresses to another idea of *direction;* and in this use it has the sense of 'going right against,' in the sense of 'striking fair and square,' or 'right in the *middle*.' Thus it gets the meaning of '*oppositeness of direction*,' and its force in 'Metánoia' is to show that the action of the mind is now to be precisely in the opposite direction to what was before the case. . . . I strongly wish I could provoke you to examine the word 'Metanoia' philologically. In its philology lie many truths. *Noia* appears to be a worn-down form for *gnoia* (compare *agnoia*, not *anoia*), and the root seems to be *gen*, meaning to beget, produce, or, as we say,

word we are drawing upon the literal elements of the compound exhaustively. We are obliged to do this because, as in the case of many other cardinal words in the New Testament, we cannot fall back upon its classical use for its scriptural definition. In the former it was often as weak an expression as our own "change of mind," and was employed in very much the same superficial way. It meant a change of perception, of opinion, of purpose, of feeling, in ordinary affairs, with the natural consequence, sometimes, of a change of action. It was a current expression for any alteration of mind or view, and for whatever retrospective emotion might attend the fact.

Its scriptural definition comes to us under very grand circumstances; the word is made

conceive. From the same root is *gennao*, to beget. *Noia (genoia)* is the begetting, shaping, or production of anything in the inner and mental world; thus all the operations or creations of the mind. The Latin *gigno, genitor, gnosco*, English 'knows,' are all from this root. The use of getting back to this philological meaning is to apply 'Metanoia' to all the operations of the mind, whether of wish, thought, or action, will, understanding, life."

over and enlarged by its environment, as if it had been reinspired and been born anew. We are compelled to seek its meaning in the abstract, native force of the compound as thus vivified by the situation in which we find it. Its history in this respect is that of the language of the New Testament.

When the Greek language, released by the conquests of Alexander the Great, three centuries and more before the Christian era, spread over the known world and became the universal language, its forms, constructions, and meanings met with curious modifications as it came in contact with the life and thought of the countries it had invaded. When in time it struck the Hebrew mind and religion at Alexandria the Septuagint translation of the Old Testament rose gradually into being; but in the act of reëxpressing ideas and principles so entirely out of the range of the Greek imagination, even that perfect and elaborate tongue mounted to a level and breathed an atmosphere it had never occupied before. It took, in many instances, a new color, a new character. There could have been no other result when the wealth of divine revelation and of the story of the only true religion was committed for recoinage to the exquisite resources of such a mint. It was now the "much-refined gold" receiving the stamp of the current common coin, but imparting to it a hitherto unknown value. Familiar words began to ring with a strange quality.[1]

If this was so, nearly three centuries before the Christian era, how must it have been when there came such a revelation to put into words, and such a revolution to put on record, as were ushered in with the Christian religion? Upon the Greek language, again, fell the burden of the new Scriptures, and this time, not by translation, but by

---

[1] The Septuagint represents only a half-way step in this assignment of the Greek language to the expression of Hebrew ideas. "The Seventy prepared the way in Greek," says Cremar, in his Preface to his "Biblico-theological Lexicon," "for the New Testament proclamation of saving truth. Fine as is their tact, it must be allowed that their language differs from that of the New Testament as the well-meant and painstaking effort of the pupils differs from the renewing and creative hand of the master." This shows itself in a less definite use of "Metánoia" than in the New Testament, where it is absolute.

direct inspiration. The pagan tongue had to wreathe itself into new phraseologies in order to give what utterance it could to ideas well-nigh unutterable. Words which had passed colloquially from mouth to mouth in the cities of Greece, words which were current in every-day speech everywhere in the world, some whose meanings had never before been profound, others whose usage had worn them thin, now rose into a significance so powerful and so sacred that they could only be used as temple-money by all ages to come. Expressions conveying a divine meaning, now most familiar to us, were occasions of astonishment to pagan and Jew alike when they were lifted into connections which transfigured them. Such, we know, were "faith," "hope," "love," "light," "truth," "life," "peace," "liberty"; such were "redemption," "atonement," "righteousness," "resurrection"; such were "Saviour" and "apostle," and many more which might be named. And such was "Metanoia." So great as this was what Schleiermacher calls "the language-moulding power of Christianity."

II.

"METÁNOIA" MISTRANSLATED "REPENTANCE."

WHEN "Metánoia" was taken up into the uses of the New Testament it came to mean, according to Archbishop Trench, "that mighty change in mind, heart, and life, wrought by the Spirit of God, *which we call repentance.*"[1]

"Which we call *repentance*"! What a *diminuendo* in the statement is here! The swelling note suddenly gives up its breath and subsides into this! It is *we*, the English-speaking world, he says, who call that "mighty change" "*repentance.*"

In other words, this is the rendering of it in our English Bible, and the accredited expression for it in all theological literature.

[1] See Trench's "Synonyms of the New Testament," p. 241, sec. lxix.

The Great Meaning of Metánoia.

Here, now, we come upon the practical and all-important point of this inquiry. For, putting these words, "Metánoia" and "*repentance*," side by side, what a radical divergency there is between them!

We are supposing the reader to be looking at the two with a perfectly fresh and unsophisticated perception. He already knows what the Greek "Metánoia" etymologically means; let us now remind him what the Latin "*repentance*" etymologically means. In its primary sense it fails to come anywhere near the other.

Its central idea is the idea of *pœnitentia*, from *pœna*, pain; suffering in view of being liable to punishment; hence grief over an act for which satisfaction might be demanded.

It would be fair to allow it also a secondary signification; suffering in view of the badness of the act itself, without regard to its consequences.

The prefix *re*, back or again, adds to this the idea of *looking back*, or *looking again*, with sorrow upon what has been done amiss.

The word thus intensively communes with the past, and represents an emotion only. This may be produced by a Change of

"Metánoia" Mistranslated "Repentance."

Mind, and it may have influence in producing a Change of Mind. It may be potentially equal to amendment of life, but it is forcing the word to put even that meaning into it, and more than forcing is necessary to make it "express that mighty Change in mind, heart, and life, wrought by the Spirit of God," which Archbishop Trench admits is the meaning of "Metánoia."

At the best it can only hang on the skirts of the great Greek expression, for *that* means a movement of the whole mind *forwards*, to which a looking backwards is only incidental. Metanoia embraces *any* consideration which may cause the Mind to "change." It implies the whole circle of influences, *repentance* among them, which may affect or mould the Mind. It necessarily brings about *repentance* as one of the results of its operation, but it brings about renewal of life as the great result of all.

In saying this we do not intend to ignore the office of *repentance* in its strict sense, nor to put that all-necessary conviction of sin which characterizes the Christian religion in any indirect relation to the Christian life.

We are only questioning the word as a rendering of "Metánoia"; as representing simply an emotion, not intellection in any way. Far back in the heart is the capacity for that emotion shut up, awaiting its proper occasions. We cannot conceive of its coming into activity unless the Mind has been already engaged, but we can conceive of the Mind being full of many processes, involving Change of thought or purpose or feeling, wherein it has not been concerned at all. In this lies its first palpable incompetency to represent so comprehensive a word.

But it may be said that it has been given a signification, theologically, which bears it into all that is equivalent to a Change of Mind, and, even further than that, to amendment of life. It has, we are told, this recognized meaning among all evangelical authorities, and is so understood by all practical Christians. If this were really so, and it had so burst the chrysalis of its etymology as to float in our consciousness arbitrarily and absolutely for as much as this, even then it were impracticable to make it compass what is meant by "Metánoia" in the New Testament. The common uses of language drag it down. It cannot sustain itself at such a height. Not only are the meshes of its origin inseparable from it, but it is too much in the web of popular speech. No word is used more loosely even by theologians, except among very careful precisians. It slips out everywhere in untechnical connections. It *will* back to its vernacular use. It *will* emerge from the popular dictionary, in its native and simple meaning, the richest and weightiest of all its familiar sisterhood of synonyms, to give force to the diction when sorrow of a godly kind is meant. Even in the Prayerbook it is convertibly employed with "*penitence*," and there is every indication that there nothing more, or not a great deal more, is intended by it.[1]

[1] A few instances, in the Prayer-book, not only of the synonymous use of "*penitence*" and "*repentance*," but also of their distinction from " amendment of life ": In the General Confession : " Restore Thou those who are *penitent*, according to Thy promises." In the larger Absolution : " Declare and pronounce, . . . being *penitent*. . . . Wherefore . . . grant us true *repentance*." In the shorter Absolution : "Promised forgiveness of sins to all those who, with *hearty repentance* and true faith, turn unto Him." In the

The Great Meaning of Metánoia.

It has proved too strong and full for this in the penitential atmosphere of the Christian life to be parted with for advanced dogmatical purposes only. Hence an element of confusion which robs it of dogmatical force.

But there is another. In the Authorized Version we find it varying about in a way that requires often considerable spiritual discernment to tell where it stands for " Metánoia," and where it does not; for there is another word, " Metaméleia,"[1] which exactly means *repentance* in its strict sense, and is also so

Litany: " Give us true *repentance*, and endue us with grace to *amend our lives.*" Collect for Ash Wednesday: " Dost forgive the sins of all those who are *penitent*, create and make in us *new and contrite* hearts." Third Ash Wednesday prayer: " Who meekly acknowledge our vileness, and truly *repent* us of our faults." In the Communion Exhortations: " If with a true *penitent* heart . . . *repent* ye truly for your sins past, have a lively and steadfast faith, . . . *amend your lives.*" " Ye who do truly *repent* . . . and *intend to lead a new life.*" In the Confession: " We acknowledge and bewail, etc. . . . We do earnestly *repent and are heartily sorry.*" In the Family Prayer: " Give them *repentance* and *better minds,*" etc.

[1] Only the verb is used in the New Testament.

rendered. This variation occurs frequently enough to make us wonder whether the translators attached any distinct doctrinal significance to it at all; and we might also be pardoned for wondering whether they were fully aware of the unique value of "Metánoia" wherever they found it.[1]

When the English Scriptures themselves do not make a distinction it can hardly be expected that theological formularies will suc-

---

[1] What are we to think, for instance, when we read that Judas "*repented himself*" (μεταμεληθεὶς); or how vivid must the peculiar sense of Metánoia—even the admitted one—have been in minds which could dismiss the following passage to be "understanded of the people"?

"For though I made you sorry with a letter, I do not *repent* [μεταμέλομαι], though I did *repent* [μεταμελόμην]. . . . Now I rejoice, not that ye were made sorry, but that ye sorrowed to *repentance* [μετάνοιαν]. . . . For godly sorrow worketh *repentance* [μετάνοιαν] to salvation not to be *repented of* [ἀμεταμέλητον]." (2 Cor. vii. 8–10.) Where is Metanoia in its lone and comprehensive grandeur here? In the original it stands nobly at the top, in the ascending scale, but not in the version. Where, too, is "evangelical *repentance*"? Certainly, in this place, not apparently above the other kind.

Judas was unquestionably equal to *repentance*, as

The Great Meaning of Metánoia.

ceed in doing so. And, moreover, as the English Bible is written in the common language of the people, and, as such, belongs to our heritage of English literature, it blends itself more with this than with the technicalities of theology; its forms of speech are popular, and what is meant by "*repentance*" in general literature, in current talk, and in dictionary definitions will necessarily be understood as intended by it. "*Repentance*" is a

people generally understand it, but was, as unquestionably, far short of Metanoia as his Master understood it. St. Paul could very naturally *repent* of having written a letter which had caused pain, and as naturally reverse the feeling when he found that sorrow had produced so substantial a thing as a Change of Mind, the condition of all others that he most valued, in which he stood himself, which, when attained, was so fixed as to be equivalent to " salvation " and was " not to be *repented of.*" And yet these two unequal words of the original are yoked under one and the same English word; and this very English word is conveniently supposed by some to bear two senses, one sense natural and the other technical!

The revisers, in this awkward passage, have translated μεταμέλομαι " regret," leaving μετάνοια to " *repentance.*" But Judas, it will be seen (Matt. xxvii. 3), still " *repents himself* "! His remorse, fruitful only of hemp, continues to be as respectably characterized,

"*Metánoia*" Mistranslated "*Repentance.*"

favorite word among all writers, especially those engaged in depicting life and action; let any one pause at it as it comes up in his general reading, and he will see what it invariably is in the consciousness of the people, and how far short, therefore, it must always fall of the biblical word " Metanoia."

But there is another and even more serious matter involved in this confusion of meaning. The use of the word "*repentance*" for

in the New Version, as if he had been " made sorry after a godly sort." So again, in Romans xi. 29, ἀμεταμέλητα is rendered " without *repentance*." (See also elsewhere.) The revisers who have kept so carefully to St. Mark's oft-repeated " straightway," for the sake of uniformity, might also have kept these words apart, throughout, for a better reason.

Dr. Roberts, in his " Companion to the Revised New Testament," speaks of these two words as " most desirable to distinguish, wherever that is possible. The one word," he says, " means simply to ' rue ' or ' regret ' a course which has been followed; the other implies that thorough *change of mind* which is implied in Christian *repentance*." But he continues (and he must be referring to the assigned or the self-imposed limitations under which the revisers labored): " Unfortunately it is not always possible to express the distinction in our language " (p. 124).

The Great Meaning of Metánoia.

"Metanoia" has thrown an almost exclusively emotional character around both the original proclamation of the gospel and its present call. Despite himself the reader hears the "*Repent ye!*" of John the Baptist and of the Saviour, like a cry, a note of danger, full of terror, amid which the hearts of the people stood still, instead of what it really was, the invocation of a mind, heart, and life which should befit such a glad and glorious "change" as the kingdom of heaven on earth. If the call had really been "*Repent ye!*" it would have been only an appeal to the feelings; and as, without question, a great deal of the call of the gospel is to the conscience where it "looks back" to what has been done amiss, and for which punishment has been incurred, it is not strange that in many quarters this supposed appeal to the *impenitent* nature only has been taken up as the burden of *all* preaching, all spiritual counsel; an appeal in their hands often wrought up with terrific penal imagery; and then the fright which has ensued and its consequences have been accepted as the change of heart.

Or, if not always so grossly mistaken, yet there is a tendency thus created to regard an emotional condition, a general passion of religious feeling, however induced, as the seat of efficacy with God, and as the only safe and promising state in which to begin and continue the Christian life.

Even more: this is sometimes considered as itself the Christian life. The result has often been the extraordinary incongruity of a life of zeal unaccompanied by a life of principle, *penitence* and faith developed in conspicuous measure in view of an *ideal* sinfulness, and the living conscience, the practical right, sunk in pharisaic forms which satisfy certain low standards of outward righteousness!

The Metanoia is not here. The profound ethical sense has not been awakened at all. Fear has no genuine ethical power. Sorrow has no sure ethical consequence. Excitement of any kind can bear, of itself, no ethical fruit. None of these can have respect with God. The only thing that can be regarded by Him is that which He has arranged everything to bring about in us: that spiritual perception of the right and the true which grows within and around a Mind that is being gradually educated up to the divine standard; the nature wide open in front, not only looking behind, and receiving the whole counsel of God, not a part of it; every faculty enlightened, every feeling inspired; the entire man engaged; conviction, not excitement; earnestness, not impulse; habitude, not paroxysm; the heart tempered by the understanding, the understanding warmed by the heart; this, the consummate and yet attainable condition, this, the Metanoia, lived alike by Master and disciple, this, the "Mind" of Christ, and made possible to all by the Spirit of God—this is not conveyed in the "*Repent ye!*" of our gospels, nor does it come within the range of much of the teaching which falls on the world's ear. The all-encompassing grandeur of an announcement which takes in the whole of life, and calls upon man to enlarge his consciousness with the eternal and the spiritual, to live on the scale of another life, to let his character grow under this great knowledge, to let his conduct fall into the lines of the revealed divine will—all this is lost.

How did such an extraordinary mistranslation get into our New Testament?

It can be attributed to what we have already hinted at, and some evidence of which we have already given, namely, a failure to grasp the comprehensive and far-reaching character of the word. It came too early in the record for the translators to perceive its transcendental level. This they easily did with some of the other words we have named, which came later, and when they had mounted the swell of the ocean on which they had embarked.

They did not catch this at once as the keynote of the New Testament, for the strain of the Old had not yet died away. And there was, besides, another music ringing in their ears: the sombre tones of a traditional theology which even the thunders of the Reformation had not drowned.

The age, too, was a Latin-speaking age. The translators read their Greek through the lenses of a language whose grain was too coarse to admit its finer spirit. The Vulgate also was an authority older than any manuscript they possessed. They could not bring themselves to render its "*Do penance*" for "Metanoeite," but they could not divest themselves of the impression of *pen-*

itence with which that rendering tinged the word.

Still they showed some signs of divergence, and it led to controversy. Beza, for instance, had revolted so far as to get his composition of "Metánoia" wrong, and make it *Metá* and *ánoia*, a change from a "want of mind," a change from "folly," and so rendered it *resipiscentia* in his Latin version—an act, however, which still showed his mental bias.[1]

We have not the authorities at hand to prove the fact, but it looks very much as if

---

[1] The reader will be interested in getting a glimpse into this controversy when it started at the opening of the Reformation. "Luther, it will be remembered, first saw the practical value of philological study when he was puzzling over the expression *pœnitentiam agite* ('*Do penance*'), which the Vulgate uses for the Greek word that in the English translation is rendered '*repent.*' Was it possible, he said to himself, that Christ and the apostles could really bid men *do penance?* Did the New Testament really stand on the side of his opponents, and of all the gross corruptions which the doctrine of *penance* had introduced? Melanchthon solved this difficulty by showing to Luther that the Greek word μετανοεῖτε, which Jerome had translated '*Do penance*,' really and etymologically meant 'Change your mind.' From that moment the Reformation entered into a conscious alliance

"*Metánoia*" Mistranslated "*Repentance.*"

the English translators, who depended so much upon Beza and his Greek text and his Latin version, were misled by the same bias and compounded "Metánoia" in the same way. If they did, it explains everything. Their "*repentance*" were a very good rendering in that case; and hence, then, the uncertain sound with which their New Testament opens to this day.

But what shall we say for the Revised Version if this be so? The revisers do not so compound it. Is it possible that so palpable a misinterpretation of the Greek has now been perpetuated because it had grown like a fossil into the substance of popular theology and so escaped recognition in the Greek as a fossil?

with the New Learning." (Professor W. Robertson Smith, "The Old Testament in the Jewish Church," Lecture II.)

The Genevan Version, a Continental and more independent one, with which the Authorized Version ran in rivalry for nearly fifty years, rendered "Metanoeîte" "Amend your lives." The Authorized itself has a marginal rendering in St. Matthew's Gospel alternative to "fruits meet for *repentance*": "answerable to amendment of life"—omitted, however, in the New Version.

The Great Meaning of Metánoia.

It may now be imagined with what interest and expectation we looked forward to the New Version, realizing full well the difficulty of reproducing the original in this place and elsewhere more faithfully, and of making a change so startling, but hoping that, *at the least*, a marginal rendering would indicate the literal alternative, or a glossarial note define the Greek expression in a way that would go far to correct the English one. But the revision flows on, making a ripple of change in almost every verse, yet with not a sign of perturbation over this sunken rock. Neither a light-ship nor a buoy warns of a spot where there has been shipwreck before now.

We understand, however, that it was the subject of discussion among the revisers, and that the matter was finally passed by, not because the present rendering was satisfactory, but because no *one* equivalent English word could be found comprehensive enough for the purpose.

What, then, has been so long lost in the Old Version, remains unrecovered in the New because of a reluctance to employ a paraphrase! The poverty of our language, in this respect, is to keep *us* poor.

"Metánoia" Mistranslated "Repentance."

Or, it may be, something else was at the bottom of it, symptoms of which are apparent in other instances. It may have been the reluctance of that kind of conservatism which prefers not to disturb traditional notions or long-established formularies.

We comfort ourselves, however, with the thought that the New Version is not a finality, but only tentative to that which shall yet meet the brave demand of the present age. What we have is, in many respects, a bold and noble move, but the whole of English Christendom is in council over the matter now, and suggestions and criticisms will flow in for some years to come; an advance in sentiment, also, will take place, making the way clearer and easier to a more fearless and absolute transfer of the original into our native tongue.

We feel prepared, at least, to say, with regard to the present point, that the necessary employment of a paraphrase should not be an occasion for hesitation in making so important an alteration. We can leave it to the candid reader to judge which is the more objectionable: a resort to a paraphrase which really translates, or the preference for a technical word, to say nothing of an uncertain one, which is *always itself in need of translation.* Better, even, were the bald phrase "Change of Mind," with an explanation which would give it fullness and dignity, than the misleading rendering we have to put up with now. There is no fear but that a nobler expression can be framed, for St. Paul himself, as we shall shortly see, found no difficulty in ringing many changes upon the idea of the word, which melt very kindly into simple English.

III.

THE INTELLECTUAL AS WELL AS MORAL COMPASS OF METÁNOIA.

So far as we have now gone we have probably done more to awaken the reader's attention to the question of the inadequacy of "*repentance*" as a rendering of "Metánoia," than to convince him that the position is rightly taken. We must go for the evidence of this to the Scriptures themselves; but, in doing so, let us recur first to our imaginary scholar whom we have supposed to be receiving his impression freshly from the original.

Happily, as it turns out, we are not obliged to go even so far as to imagine such a scholar, for the impressions of an actual one of that kind came recently to our hand, which are in such singular coincidence with the view we are trying to present that we venture to quote them entire. We are glad, also, to avail our-

The Great Meaning of Metánoia.

selves of his brief dissertation as a guide in directing a part of the inquiry.

That accomplished master of Greek, De Quincey (who, if any one ever did, held his mind clear and free in a scholarly consciousness of the transcendent atmosphere into which the Greek language rose when it was summoned to meet the necessities of Christian truth and the exigencies of divine inspiration), was, it seems, actually confronted by an intelligent friend with the very question which is now engaging us. The record of it will be found in his "Autobiographic Sketches."[1]

"Lady Carbury," he writes, "one day told me that she could not see any reasonable ground for what is said of Christ, and else-

---

[1] "He [De Quincey] passed through a number of schools and . . . was distinguished for his eminent knowledge of Greek. At fifteen he was pointed out by his master (himself a ripe scholar) to a stranger in the remarkable words: 'That boy could harangue an Athenian mob better than you or I could address an English one.' . . . In this, as in the subtlety of the analytical power, De Quincey must have strongly resembled Coleridge." (Harriet Martineau, "Biographical Sketches," p. 95.)

where of John the Baptist, that He opened His mission by preaching '*repentance.*' Why '*repentance*'? Why then, more than at any other time? Her reason for addressing this remark to me was that she feared there might be some error in the translation of the Greek expression. I replied that, in my opinion, there was, and that I had myself always been irritated by the entire irrelevance of the English word, and by something very like cant, on which the whole burden of the passage is thrown. How was it any natural preparation for a vast spiritual revelation that men should, first of all, acknowledge any special duty of *repentance?* The *repentance*, if any movement of that nature could be intelligently supposed called for, should more naturally follow this great revolution—which as yet, both in its principle and in its purpose, was altogether mysterious—than herald it or ground it. *In my opinion the Greek word 'Metánoia' concealed a most profound meaning—a meaning of prodigious compass—which bore no allusion to any ideas whatever of repentance.* The *Metá* carried with it an emphatic expression of its original idea—the idea of transfer, of translation; or, if we prefer a Grecian to a Roman appareling, the idea of a *metamorphosis*. And this idea, to what is it applied? Upon what object is the idea of spiritual transfiguration made to bear? Simply upon the noëtic or intellectual faculty—the faculty of shaping and conceiving things under their true relations. The holy herald of Christ, and Christ Himself, the Finisher of prophecy, made proclamation alike of the same mysterious summons, as a baptism or rite of initiation, namely, Μετανοεῖτε: Henceforth transfigure your theory of moral truth; the old theory is laid aside as infinitely insufficient; a new and spiritual revelation is established. Metanoeïte! Contemplate moral truth as radiating from a new center; apprehend it under transfigured relations.

"John the Baptist, like other earlier prophets, delivered a message which, probably enough, he did not himself more than dimly understand, and never in its full compass of meaning. Christ occupied another station. Not only was He the original Interpreter, but He was Himself the Author—Founder at once, and Finisher—of the great transfiguration applied to ethics, which He and the Baptist alike announced as forming

Intellectual Compass of Metánoia.

the code of the new revolutionary era now opening its endless career. The human race was summoned to bring a transfiguring sense and spirit of interpretation (Metanoia) to a transfigured ethics; an altered organ to an altered object. This is by far the grandest miracle recorded in Scripture. No exhibition of blank power—not the arresting of the earth's motion, not the calling back of the dead to life—can approach in grandeur to this miracle which we daily behold, namely, the inconceivable mystery of having written and sculptured upon the tablets of man's heart a new code of moral distinctions, all modifying—many reversing—the old ones. What would have been thought of any prophet if he should have promised to transfigure the celestial mechanics; if he had said, 'I will create a new pole-star, a new zodiac, and new laws of gravitation; briefly, I will make a new earth and new heavens'? And yet a thousand times more awful it was to undertake the writing of new laws upon the spiritual conscience of man. 'Metanoeïte!' was the cry from the wilderness. Wheel into a new center your moral system; *geocentric* has that system been up to this hour, that is, having earth and the earthly for its starting-point; henceforth make it *heliocentric*, that is, with the sun, or the heavenly, for the principle of motion."[1]

This brilliant statement we believe to be true as far as it goes; but the heralding was not all a bare summons. It was accompanied by every credential which the Summoner could show; not only the credential of signs and wonders, but of teachings, which evidently inclosed far more than was apparent, which held out an ulterior meaning to be disclosed in due time; teachings which penetrated to the very soul, and moved the heart of the age wherever they were heard.

[1] De Quincey's works, "Autobiographic Sketches," vol. i., p. 434.
In a closing note to the " Supplementary Essay on the Essenes," he recurs to the subject again: " Metánoia—which word, I contend, cannot properly be translated '*repentance*'; for it would have been pure cant to suppose that age, or any age, as more under a summons to *repentance* than any other assignable. I understand by Metánoia a revolution of thought— a great intellectual change—in the accepting a new centre for all moral truth from Christ; which center it was that subsequently caused all the offense of Christianity to the Roman people."

"Metánoia" was the theme—the *programma*—projected, and everything that was afterwards spoken wrought out its meaning upon the mind of the time, sensibly or insensibly preparing and making ready its way. It was the great harbinger word of the Gospel, bearing witness to the "Light." So, while, as De Quincey says, it was a prodigious assumption, the assumption of a power to work the most stupendous of miracles, it, at the same time, assumed the capacity in man to make the miracle possible. Christ would wait for the word to tell. This was His method throughout, even in special instances. For example: "Destroy this temple," said He, at the very outset, to those who questioned His authority to expel the traders, "and in three days I will raise it up." It was only after Pentecost that the evangelist was able to add, "He spake of the temple of His body." But just as that declaration sank into their minds and worked unconsciously there—indeed, worked in the minds of some of them till it reappeared three years after as one of the taunts flung up at Him on the cross: "Thou that destroyest the temple, and buildest it in three days, save Thyself"—so the summons to a mysterious Metanoia must have kept their whole consciousness thrilled with the sense of a strange experience, and as strange expectation, dumb and unintelligible, perhaps, but preparing the ground for what was to be sown in it.

What could have helped a great scheme of progress better than to put a word of prophecy at the beginning of it? What could have helped the teacher more than a preliminary word which was equivalent to an inspiration in its power to stir every fibre and create a boundless desire to learn and to know? Such an all-permeating word was like the slow fusion of the metal for the mould and the slow cooling of it while it was assuming a new form. It was proclaiming a Change of Mind, and creating it at the same moment, by drawing the subject of it into active and intelligent participation.

De Quincey has given the weight of his authority, as a scholar, to the *intellectual* bearing of the word "Metánoia," in the extraordinary use to which it is applied in the New Testament. But he might have included in his statement its equal and coincident range in the sphere of the moral and affectional nature. *Noūs*, as we have already said, corresponds perfectly to "Mind." It allows our conception of an intellectual consciousness to let itself down into the whole possible profundity of a spiritual consciousness. This is, perhaps, implied in what he says, and it is as well that the stress was laid by him on the intellectual character of the expression, inasmuch as this is the very point that is most in danger of being lost sight of, and is of vast importance in any complete consideration of the subject.

The office of the intellect in the apprehension of divine truth is not given its due consequence. "The noëtic faculty, or the faculty of shaping and conceiving things under their true relations," to use De Quincey's expression, is foremost in all human action—it is *first*. The fact of the dependence of our whole nature upon it is almost too palpable to dwell upon, and yet the instantaneous flash with which outward things sometimes pass through it into the heart often leads us to ignore the office of the medium by which they entered.

Take a common instance of this unconsciousness. The hymn which, as it is sung, suffuses the soul with religious emotion has gone, in less than the twinkling of an eye, through a full and varied intellectual process of which the soul has taken no notice. First, the perception of its meaning; next, the perception of its beauty as an expression of the meaning to the degree that sensibility is excited; next, the susceptibility to its musical rendering, which intensifies the sensibility; next, the throng of associations which comes, partly from the memory, partly from the imagination, and, like the legendary angel of Bethesda, stirs the waters of feeling welling up beneath—these are purely intellectual. We are hardly aware, unless we watch the mechanism of our nature, how much and how continually the *Noûs*, in its primary sense, is occupied in conveying inspiration to the heart. Memory is forever pouring its store into this realm; knowledge of every kind is daily streaming in by the portals of the senses, passing through the strangest transmutations as it is touched by the reason or the fancy, till it reaches the sanctuary and mounts into something which takes hold of the entire nature. But *then* the first has become the last, and the last first. That only which reaches, engrosses, and moves the *heart* is that which works into the essence of the life; and that which remains intellectual alone is only on the way to its practical end, an abortive thing if it gets no farther.

The intellect may be the Beautiful Gate—even, literally, Solomon's Porch—but the heart is the vital centre, the Sanctuary of the temple. All the outer courts point towards this, the precinct of the spirit. It is only when the thoughts which throng them like the multitude, it is only when the purposes which minister in them like the priests, have actually lit the altar-fire and gone behind the veil, that the divine uses of the temple are manifested and make their return. And yet it is none the less true that without these courts of approach the altar would never burn, the hidden power within would never be evoked.

It is the intellect which awakens that inmost interior. It receives the crowd in its magnificent areas, it reports the situation outside, and then the secret heart, brooded upon by the Spirit of God, takes in the situation; the mystic circuit is complete; upon that heartfelt consciousness the character is formed, and upon that character the life. It is a divine dependence ordained in the structure of our nature, and the process of it ought to be vividly before our minds if we would understand the operation of the Metanoia.

We have used this apostolic figure of the "temple of God" not only to give as graphic illustration as possible to a manifold fact of our nature under any circumstances, but also to consecrate the fact to the sacred relation in which we are discussing it, and bring it, besides, into the very connection in which St. Paul used the metaphor.

It is only when the situation is a divine one that man is found to be the temple of God. So long as he confronts only the spirit of the world, whether it be in the nature of things or in the nature of men, he is like Herod's temple, without the Shechinah. He is only in partial use; his true occupation is gone, or has not come. But when "the Lord visits His temple," then the wisdom of the world finds no longer entrance, but "the wisdom of God in a mystery." In *that* change of situation comes the wondrous Change of Mind.

"Eye hath not seen," exclaims the Apostle, "nor ear heard, neither have entered into the heart of man, the things which God hath prepared for them that love Him"—not in the next world only, but in this. "Now," he continues, "we have received, not the spirit of the world, but the Spirit which is of God; that we might *know* the things that are freely given to us of God." "Know ye not that ye are the temple of God, and that the Spirit of God dwelleth in you? . . . Let no man deceive himself. If any man among you seemeth to be wise in this world, let him become a fool, that he may be wise." Such was to be the utter dispossession of himself, such the utter evacuation of the wisdom of the world, such the Metanoia, when he came to know "Christ the power of *God*, and the wisdom of *God*."

St. Paul, when charged with a message like this, may well have scorned to come with the "excellency of speech or of wisdom" which then captivated the imagination of men; but no man ever lived who, "in demonstration of the Spirit and of power," made a greater appeal to the intellect, more riveted the intelligent attention of the world, and more elicited the admiration of the finest intellects the world has known. If ever a man was chosen because of his intellectual power, and if ever a man appealed to the understanding and struck home through every faculty and intuition which the understanding could summon, it was he.

IV.

THE INAUGURAL ACTION OF METÁNOIA IN THE FIRST AGE.

IF we have made our meaning clear—and much that we have said has an ulterior reference which will make it clearer—the reader is now prepared to take up the historic moment when the gospel was inaugurated, and to contemplate the stupendous change of outward situation which then ensued.

What an epoch it was! What a meaning lay in the Metanoia that was then proclaimed! "The noëtic faculty, or the faculty of shaping and conceiving things under their true relations," entered now upon its work, and the issue was to be a revolution in the whole human conception of life. Christ substituted His own wisdom for the wisdom of the world, and what we see recorded in the New Testament is, first, the natural process of the

The Great Meaning of Metánoia.

Metanoia—this wisdom working through the intelligence upon the heart, the conscience, and the life; and, next, the thoroughness of the result in forming a new spiritual consciousness in that age.[1]

It was, indeed, the "beginning of miracles": the water was turned into wine. What else could have taken place from His presence at the bridal where heaven and earth were made one? The change was now inevitable from the lower into the higher, from the temporal into the eternal, from the natural into the spiritual, from the human into the divine. Life took a new character and another meaning when He drew near. It was found to be His life. The letter of the Old Testament dissolved into the spirit of the New. The law disappeared, and the righteousness which is by faith, red as the blood of a great Sacrifice, was found instead, filling the vessels of human purification to the brim. The good wine had been kept until now!

Did ever the world see so mighty and so radical a revolution as came upon it then?

[1] See Matthew Arnold's view of "Metánoia" in a note at the end of the Essay.

Judaism gave way to a universal religion. The Mosaic night broke into the dawn of the perfect day. The Fatherhood of God was revealed to all men, and a brotherhood with the Son of God! Now were they the sons of God! partakers of the divine nature! This world was discovered to be within the boundaries of the other world, and death was merged into a resurrection of the dead! Righteousness and truth were to prevail, for the power of sin had been destroyed! And the efficacy of all this lay in the person of the Christ. It was He who gave all this light. The order of human life reversed itself in Him. All conduct was to flow from a spirit within, not by a law without. Selfishness was turned into self-surrender and self-sacrifice. The affections were to be set upon things above, not on things on the earth. The spirit was everything, the flesh profited nothing. In all human action was to be the consciousness of Eternity; in all intercourse of man with man no less than the magnanimity of God.

As we said in the beginning, what strikes us first, as we open our New Testament, is

The Great Meaning of Metánoia.

the commanding position in which we find the word "Metánoia." It is the great initiatory word of the first three gospels. However they may vary in the way they begin the story, they unite in the way they introduce this. The summons to mankind, first by the Baptist, next by the Christ, is to a Metanoia —a Change of Mind. And when we come to the fourth gospel, with its interior view of the life of Christ, it is to discover "Metanoia" also at the very outset, but in another form: in an expression which, characteristically of that gospel, carries us into the very depths of the selfsame idea.

Let us combine the four accounts. Now we shall see it in its true perspective; that is, successively in its intellectual, ethical, and spiritual development.

In the very beginning we have the Christ, half philosophically, half spiritually depicted as the "Lógos," the "Word"; then as the "Light of men." What greater implication could there be that Christianity was directed through the understanding to the heart? Next, John the Baptist is spoken of as the "witness" to this Light. He was to "go before the face of the Lord to prepare His way." The method of his preparation was to produce, first, a powerful, controlling impression upon the intelligence of the people. His personal appearance, his clothing like that of an ancient prophet, his ascetic look, his secluded life, the "voice," out of Isaiah, with which he spoke, the burden of his first announcement—all were in keeping, and were calculated to rouse the whole nation. The past came vividly back to their memory; the future was as vividly, though mysteriously and presagingly, brought to their imagination. He came "proclaiming a Baptism of Metanoia unto sending away [1] of sins." His vocal summons was that of a herald. "Metanoeîte! Take a New Mind upon you: for the

---

[1] εἰς ἄφεσιν, *áphesis*, a sending away, a letting go, a setting free. The Latin "remission," a sending back, as used in the English versions, savors too much of a *letting off*, and is too evidently a rendering colored by its association with the punitive element in *repentance*. Metanoia is "unto the *sending away* of sins." That is, its natural effect is to set the soul free from the bondage of the disposition to sin.

But Christ, in creating the Metanoia, *takes away* sin. It is His personal work.

The Great Meaning of Metánoia.

Kingdom of Heaven is at hand." And, as if his "voice" were not enough, he spoke also by this symbol whose meaning must have been universally understood to be a change from an old condition into a new, even such a change, as they esteemed it, as that from dark paganism to glorious Judaism. It now meant a change from dark Judaism to some far exceeding glory. It meant a change that would really, not typically, bring with it a sending away of sins. He thus expressively coupled this sign of a Change of Condition with his summons to a Change of Mind. It was no other than "a Baptism of Metanoia."

His summons of the Pharisees and Sadducees to a Change of Mind was as revolutionary and as radical as it well could be. In this he struck right at their views. He broke their illusions. "Think not to say within yourselves, We have Abraham to our father: for I say unto you, That God is able of these stones to raise up children unto Abraham. Even now the ax is lying at the root of the trees." There must be fruit worthy of the Metanoia (τῆς μετανοίας).

The effect of these utterances upon the people was as distinctly intellectual as it was emotional. Their whole intelligence was roused to such a degree that they not only went down into the Baptism and sought practical counsel for their future lives, but they were thrown into a state of "expectation." They were excited to inquiry. "All men reasoned in their hearts of John, whether *he* were the Christ, or not." Finally priests and Levites came down from Jerusalem to ask him, "Who art thou? that we may give an answer to them that sent us. What sayest thou of thyself?"

Up to a certain point he had not announced the Christ, but he *had* awakened every thought and association which could suggest Him. He would seem to have gathered this intense concentration of attention upon himself in order to acquire additional power in portraying the greater grandeur of Him who was coming.

He made himself the dark background of the picture he now drew. He himself was but a voice. "One mightier than I cometh." He himself was not worthy to stoop down and unlace His sandals. "I indeed baptize you in water; but He shall baptize you in the Holy Spirit and fire." He is the real Baptizer; the Metanoia that is to come by Him is to come through the Spirit of God, and something more potent than water. With Him *that* Baptism and the Metanoia are one. "What I am, what I teach, what I summon you to, what I baptize in, are but foreshadows of Him."

Powerful as was this picture, John drew still another. It was based upon a familiar scene in their every-day life. This Coming One was the great Harvester, whose winnowing-fork should stir humanity to its depths, as so much grain on the threshing-floor, and throw it against the currents of the Spirit. The wheat would fall at His feet and go into His garner, but the stubble would fly beyond Him to become only fuel for fire.

He painted these two strong pictures upon their imaginations—pictures whose parabolic force would sink profoundly into their minds. Vague conceptions were they as yet—as vague as the idea of a Metanoia itself must have been—but there was a far-reaching significance in them which, as now united with the call to a Change of Mind, time would reveal and the reality would confirm.

Inaugural Action of Metánoia in the First Age.

The seed of much thinking was sown, and a kind of thinking that was sure to work its way into the life.

It was not until after all this; not until Jesus had come and been baptized; not, indeed, until He had returned to him after the temptation in the wilderness—that John made known the fact that his own Baptism had had a still deeper purpose than had yet been suspected. Not only was it a sign of the Metanoia in view of the impending Change, not only did it convey a typical intimation of Him who should bring about this Change, but it had all along been the designed occasion when the Christ Himself, in bodily presence, should be made known.

John had been utterly in the dark as to who He was. He had been in even a greater state of expectation than the people. All he knew was that "He that sent him to baptize in water, the same had said to him, Upon whomsoever thou shalt see the Spirit descending, and remaining upon Him, the same is He who baptizeth in the Holy Spirit." "I knew Him not," he said afterwards; "but in order that [*ἵνα*] He should be made manifest unto Israel, for this cause came I [διὰ τοῦτο ἦλθον ἐγὼ] baptizing in water."

This remarkable statement cannot be too strongly reiterated in view of the significance we may attach to it. The symbol, Baptism, was put into John's hands not only, as we say, to express the impending Metanoia, the Change of Mind to which the people were summoned, but also to be the means by which the Christ, the consummate Agent of it all, should be made known to John himself and to the people. Everything was in suspense until this supreme moment of perception, knowledge, realization, came. The Metanoia was not at the full until *He* was "made manifest."

The fact further defines the word. John's own Mind was waiting to be informed. The Mind of Israel was waiting to be informed. Both were yet in the Pronoia. They were in the line of that information, but the knowledge had not come. They stood on the verge of the Metanoia. When it should dawn it would affect every Mind according to its previous condition. The Change would be either an evolution or a revolution; but in

Inaugural Action of Metánoia in the First Age.

either case it would be a Change of Mind, an advance into a new stage of consciousness, a confirmation of what had already been dimly discerned, or a contradiction of what had hitherto been wrongly imagined. The one was John's position, ready for any development; the other, in different degrees and forms, was the position of the people.

Let it still be borne in mind that this was known as "a Baptism of Metanoia." Now Jesus Himself was to enter the rite. If it were "the Baptism of *repentance*," as it is rendered, why was He there? What had it to do with Him, or He with it? This has been the puzzle of theologians, who labor under the prepossession of the old rendering. But that He should participate in and be the central glory of "a Baptism of a Change of Mind," in the large sense in which we understand that expression, would be sublimely consistent with His character as the Christ; and it would, moreover, give us an inner glimpse of His life, which would ally it still more with our own.

We have reason to think that Jesus Himself was in the background with the others, personally known to John, yet spiritually unknown to him; personally known to many, yet spiritually undiscerned by them; personally known to Himself in the deepest consciousness of what He might be, perceiving in Himself all the marks of the Christ, yet with that consciousness awaiting the seal of the divine confirmation. Israel, John, Jesus, were all, in these different degrees, in the Pronoia—the Mind before it had crossed into perfect intelligence. The "Baptism of Metanoia" was therefore to be the manifestation of Christ *to Himself* as well as to them.[1]

The event declares this to be the very fact. "When all the people had been baptized," then He also entered by the selfsame heaven-appointed gate—it was "of heaven," not "of men"—into the new order of things: the Kingdom of Heaven which was at hand. What

[1] Was there no meaning in the event when, after three years of this transfiguring experience, suddenly "the fashion of His countenance was altered, and His face did shine as the sun," to a group of His disciples on the mount, and the divine words uttered at His Baptism were uttered again? Was there no meaning in it when the whole truth and reality of that vision of a *change* burst upon all of them in His resurrection from the dead?

Inaugural Action of Metánoia in the First Age.

happened? As He came up out of the water the heavens were rent asunder, "and lo, a voice from heaven, saying, Thou art—this is—My beloved Son, in whom I am well pleased." "And I saw," said John, "and bare record that this is the Son of God."[1]

What a Metanoia was there, to both Jesus and John! The Pronoia was over with both! The boundary had been crossed; the veil had been lifted. The whole great advance had been made in a moment of time. Jesus, filled with the immensity of a now confirmed consciousness, "filled with the Spirit," went into the wilderness to breast the trial which

---

[1] "By this anointing of the Spirit," says Olshausen, "the gradual development of the *human* consciousness in Jesus attained its height. . . . The Baptism, accordingly, was the sublime season when the character of the χριστός, which was dormant in the gradually developing child and youth, now came forth and expanded itself. Compare the remarkable words in Justin, 'Dial. Tryph. cum Jud.,' p. 226: 'Though the Messiah has been born and lives, He is unknown, and does not even know Himself, nor has any power, until Elias shall come and anoint Him and make Him known to all.'" (Olshausen's "Commentary on the New Testament," vol. i., p. 271.)

should come to Him as the announced Son of God. John emerged from the wilderness into the full light of the same Metanoia, into the blaze of the very consummation amid which he was to wane out of sight, to await the return of Jesus, and to say, "Behold the Lamb of God! This is He of whom I spake."

And what a Metanoia had come, also, upon the disciples of John and upon Israel! With Jesus and with John the Change of Mind, as we say, was in the form of development, an evolution from one state of consciousness into another. But upon Israel it had come like a Change from darkness to light, from ignorance to knowledge, a revolution of consciousness, an inversion, as time went on, of all that they had ever thought or believed or felt.

But let us return to the great final scene at the Baptism, which shed its splendor over the rite.

The virtue never left it which entered it then. Henceforth it was consecrated into a sacrament, forever allied with a Change of Mind and of Life. Baptism, as it once de-

Inaugural Action of Metanoia in the First Age.

fined the Metanoia, was always to define it. For go now from the first three gospels into the fourth. What do we find there—also in the outset of the record? We hear our Lord discoursing of a New Birth—a birth from Above (ἄνωθεν), a birth of the Spirit, and this as accompanying a birth of water!

Even as it had been with the Master, so was it to be with the disciple. The full revelation of sonship in God was to break upon *him*, also, after he had ascended through the outward rite. Then the Spirit would meet the Mind openly, and renew it day by day. It also was to Change as it learned, as it was tempted, and as it suffered.

Where is the harmony of the gospels, where is the harmony of the Gospel itself, unless the "Baptism of Metanoia" proclaimed by John the Baptist to the people was the same as the "born of water and of the Spirit" announced by Jesus to Nicodemus?

So here, in the profoundest of the gospels, we have the profoundest exposition of the word.

V.

METANOIA THE METHOD OF CHRIST'S TEACHING.

WE are now fairly brought to the moment when Jesus Himself began to proclaim and to say, "The time is fulfilled, and the Kingdom of God is at hand: Metanoeite! Take upon you a New Mind, and Believe the Glad Tidings."

What a new and concentrated light falls upon the life of Christ if we look upon it as the process or action of creating the Metanoia! With this single idea in view His whole method comes definitely before us. It was all comprised in the terms of the above announcement: "The divine epoch of the world has come! God is now to reign on earth! Heaven is all about you! Sin, sorrow, death, are no more! Peace, joy, eternal life, are yours! The night is far spent;

the day is at hand. Awake, awake! All is changed! Change *ye!* Believe not the world; believe *Me!* I bring you good tidings of great joy!"

Supernatural as this revelation was, it was, like Him who brought it, subject to the order of nature in human nature when delivered to mankind. That order, as we have said, is this: all inward "change" proceeds from outward "change." A change of outward situation induces a change of mental consciousness; a change of mental consciousness induces a change of moral disposition; a change of moral disposition induces a change of outward life. *Give a man a new consciousness and he will develop a new nature.*

Upon this natural order of the Metanoia did Christ proceed. He first revealed a change of circumstance. He filled the soul with knowledge altogether new. He communicated to it ideas and inspired it with principles which brought about it the horizon of another world. Then, step by step, came the dispossession of the old nature till it had reached the vital center, the seat of the conscience and the will, and then, step by step, the moral transformation began. It was "the expulsive power of a new affection." The "world" was cast out like a deaf and blind spirit, and the once divine heart was left cleansed and free. And this was done, as we say, by occupying, first, the intellectual nature of man, by engaging the whole power of his understanding *with the Truth*. But the nature of that truth was such that it struck through to the heart; for "truth" and "righteousness," in His mouth, meant the same thing. Like the hymn we hear, the intellectual process, however full, was unnoticed in the greater fullness of the spiritual impression produced. It came from Him on fire with the vividness of His own consciousness, and its illumination, as well as its inspiration, was thrown through these out-looking windows into the inmost chambers of the spirit. But these intellectual windows were the first to blaze under the light that poured into them. His opening summons to the Metanoia was addressed to the intelligence, and without an awakened intelligence it could not have moved the people as it did. All His subsequent preaching then became an education, an education by gradual revelation. He was

Metanoia the Method of Christ's Teaching.

known as the "Teacher." He called His followers His "disciples"—learners. "Every one," He said, "that hath learned of the Father cometh unto Me." "Hearken unto Me every one of you, and understand." "Perceive ye not, neither understand?" "All things that I have heard of My Father I have made known unto you." His constant formula was, "He that hath ears to hear, let him hear!" which applied as much to the interest felt by the intelligence as to the disposition that lay in the will.

His mode of teaching involved almost every form of arresting attention and producing an impression.

He portrayed the Kingdom of Heaven in parables of the most diverse description; some so plain as to clear up a whole situation; some so obscure as to hold in reserve a lesson, of which time would develop the meaning; some with intimations so vast, so stupendous, that the heaven and the earth seemed passing away.

He spoke, sometimes, in startling enigmas which roused thought, conjecture, speculation, inquiry; sometimes in language as startling for its hyperbole, in order to vivify to the utmost an essential truth; sometimes, again, in precepts so plain that the very children could understand them.

Sometimes He spoke in statements which, like those to the woman of Samaria, widened as into infinitude the local horizon about Mount Gerizim or Jerusalem; which, like those in the Sermon on the Mount, revealed the divine profundities under the law and under all human life.

He employed reasoning and argument. He appealed to the imagination; He struck indelible pictures upon the memory.

He was ever speaking of the "Truth." Even at the last He declared to Pilate that "to this end was He born, and for this cause came He into the world, that He should bear witness unto the Truth."

His whole endeavor seemed to be to develop the capacity for Belief; and when it was developed it took the mental-ethical-spiritual name of "Faith"—another Greek word elevated into a transcendental meaning, and expressing the idea of Metanoia in its highest, most concentrated, most effectual form.

He used every credential which He brought with Him to fasten His personality upon the age, and to make Himself a vivid and memorable, as well as a lovable, presence forever. Every sign and wonder was worked as much to prove His origin and authority as to express His loving-kindness and tender mercy.

He was the Sower who went out to sow. He left in that soil principles working, ideas germinating, thoughts springing, as well as feelings moved and affections stirred, the issues of which that soil very imperfectly comprehended until the ripening moment had come.

He threw a mystical shadow over life which was to deepen into an eclipse of all that was earthly. He set forward the boundaries of this world into the other world, and brought into this life the spirit of the heavenly life, the spirit of eternity amid things temporal. He revealed the existence of the absolute Right, the near presence of the love and of the will of God.

With His disciples it was a constant, a growing Metanoia. At first they were full of joy, of anticipation, of triumph. They were not to fast: the Bridegroom was with them. The sombre word "*repentance*" were sadly inadequate to express all that He had created. Doubtless, here and there, some, like Peter, astonished by this exhibition of power, fell down at His knees, saying, "Depart from me; for I am a sinful man, O Lord;" or some, like Zaccheus, also powerfully impressed, offered the fullest reparation for an evil life; or some, like the woman that was a sinner, loved much because they had been forgiven much. Such results were the inevitable, as they were the designed, consequence of His personal influence, and, sooner or later, they were to come upon all. But the influence *began* in the intellect awakened; the intellect overwhelmed with a new perception, which grew into a new conviction, into a belief in His authority, and a belief in what He revealed.

And, as if to indicate to His disciples that the Metanoia was even then by no means complete, He told them at the close that "He had yet many things to say unto them, but that they could not bear them now. Howbeit when He, the Spirit of Truth,

Metanoia the Method of Christ's Teaching.

should come, He would guide them into all Truth." "He should bring all things to their *remembrance*, whatsoever He Himself had said unto them."

And, indeed, the Metanoia had not fully come. So little had they comprehended, so much in them still lay latent, that His death was a catastrophe which ended all their hope. Their Metanoia entered upon a new stage when He rose from the dead. Their "sorrow was turned into joy," as He had predicted. But even then the consummate hour had not come, .and even then they could not have fully taken in His last injunction "that Metanoia unto sending away of sins should be proclaimed in His name," that they should "go and make learners of all the nations, Baptizing them in the name of the Father, and of the Son, and of the Holy Spirit."

The Metanoia was not complete until the hour when the prophecy of John the Baptist was literally fulfilled; until the Christ Himself was, so to speak, complete; until He came again, "Baptizing them in the Holy Spirit

The Great Meaning of Metánoia.

and fire;" until, as the great Harvester, He thrust His winnowing-fork into the harvest He had planted, and cast it against the wind of that Spirit, thoroughly to purge His floor.

Then, in the outburst of that mighty wind, came the Metanoia complete—complete so far as it was an instant realization—upon the disciples, upon the age. The whole original impression of Him revived, and a deeper than that impression was inspired. The world went into shadow. The Kingdom of Heaven was on earth. They had "the Mind of Christ."

But what was its first manifestation? A public phenomenon on the day of Pentecost. There was a vocal outburst of divine ecstasy. Whether they spoke in languages or in mystical utterances, it was the release of their pent-up souls when the full realization came upon them.

The multitude cried in wonder, as they saw and heard, "What meaneth this?" or in mockery, "These men are full of new wine!" Their amazement and skepticism were equally met by an illuminating speech from Peter: a statement of facts, an argument from prophecy, irresistibly concentrated upon the event which had shaken Jerusalem fifty days before; a speech which leaped from the supreme Metanoia of the moment and carried all its impalpable power into the minds before him. The same light then broke upon them.

"Men! brethren!" they exclaimed, "what shall we do?"—the very words of the multitudes to John the Baptist when all this was foreshadowed; and then they heard again the burden of the Baptist and of the Christ: "Μετανοήσατε! Take a New Mind, and be Baptized every one of you in the name of Jesus Christ."

The same thing occurred when, shortly afterwards, a miracle was performed. There was another convincing statement, with the same exhortation. Observe the antithesis:

"I wot that through ignorance [ἄγνοιαν] ye did it. . . . Μετανοήσατε! Take a New Mind therefore, and be converted, that your sins may be blotted out, so that [ὅπως] times of refreshing may come from the presence of the Lord."

How little the *repent* of our version takes in the compass of the counsel! They had *repented* already, in the usual sense;

The Great Meaning of Metánoia.

they were deeply *penitent*, they were "pricked to the heart." But Peter made them understand that compunction or any other like feeling was not all. Their Minds must seize the new situation, so that God might send Him who was before proclaimed to them, Jesus Christ. They were to turn from ignorance to knowledge.

VI.

THE METANOIA OF ST. PAUL—FAITH AND RENEWAL.

AND now one other stage, which will carry us even deeper into the Scriptural aspect of this subject.

If ever there was an instance of Metanoia under all the conditions which could exhibit the fullest import of the word it was that of what is inadequately called the "conversion" of St. Paul.

It would almost seem as if the Change of Mind in a man of such personal greatness, moral strength, and conspicuous record had been brought about in the sudden, public way it was in order to put into a concentrated form, and reveal on the grandest scale, a process and a fact which in ordinary cases could not be so visibly represented. We have here in colossal proportions, and, potentially, in a moment of time, the Metanoia of which all Christian experience is made. That such a thing could and did take place in the case of a man of this intelligence has been cited as one of the strongest evidences of the Christian religion. What he was before the Change we know:

First of all, one of the most richly endowed intellects and one of the most powerful natures ever known among men. Following upon that, intensified by his proud Judaism, by his narrow Pharisaism, by his profound knowledge of Jewish law and traditions, by his devotion to the religion of his fathers, he turned out a zealot in the cause of Judaism, so dark, bigoted, and bloody as to make him a leader in the persecution of the new faith. He had proved impenetrable to the story and teaching of Jesus, to the accounts of His miracles, even to the signs and wonders wrought in His name by the apostles.

But in the very hour when his Mind was most turbulent, vengeful, and determined, Jesus meets him in the way. As soon as the conviction of his error had broken upon his Mind, as visibly as the great light which had blinded his eyes, his first inquiry was, like all previous disciples, " What must I do ? "

" I have appeared unto thee for this purpose," answered Jesus, " to make thee a minister and a witness both of these things which thou hast seen, and *of those things in the which I will appear unto thee;* delivering thee from the people, and from the Gentiles, unto whom now I send thee, *to open their eyes, and to turn them from darkness to light.*"

" Whereupon," St. Paul says, " I was not disobedient unto the heavenly vision ; but showed unto them that they should Take upon them a New Mind [μετανοεῖν] and turn to God, and do works worthy of the Metanoia [ἄξια τῆς μετανοίας]."

When the scales had fallen from his eyes his Mind beheld no other vision than of Christ. He that had then met him was thenceforth ever before him. The narrow, prejudiced, sectarian Pharisee was "changed" into an apostle of Christianity so magnificent, so enlightened, so large and liberal in his conception of it, that none of his new brethren could keep pace with him, as even all present ecclesiasticism is in danger of falling behind him.

The Great Meaning of Metánoia.

All the marks of the Metanoia are here:

It was the Mind changed through circumstance; for when he beheld the supernatural presence of the Lord, as actually risen from the dead, the whole vision of his error burst upon him.

It was the Mind changed in understanding; for he spent three years of solitude in Arabia, receiving the fullest indoctrination from Christ.

It was the Mind changed by evolution; for, with the root of the matter in him, he now grasped entirely the transcendent change of situation, and came forth able, above all others, to reconcile the old economy with the new, to proclaim the advanced principles of the Gospel with a profundity of spiritual discernment which no one should ever exceed, and to be the most powerful advocate Christianity should ever know.

It was the Mind changed in disposition; for, from the fierce, proud, intolerant, self-sufficient son of the law, he became the patient, humble, compassionate, affectionate servant of Christ, "all things to all men."

It was the Mind changed by development; for the same capacity for faith, for zeal, for force and energy, for religious devotion, was now carried over and enlarged in the interest of a cause as new and as vast as the whole just revealed purpose of God in man.

It was the Mind changed by revolution; for it was a revolt from Judaism in its narrow rabbinical form, a total break with the artificial, superstitious, selfish system under which he had been born and bred, and a leap into the large spiritual consciousness of Christ Himself.

It was the Mind changed before *repentance* set in, which *repentance* accompanied, which *repentance* intensified, which *repentance* helped to fill with a due apprehension of the cross, but of the extent of whose growth in its change, of the extent of whose apprehension of his Lord, the word "*repentance*" in its fullest theological acceptation could never follow, compass, or describe. Nothing less than the word "Metanoia"—or some English expression that shall be the full equivalent of the word—can compass or describe it. For what was its most conspicuous, foremost feature? A profoundly illuminated intelligence followed by a nature as profoundly penetrated. The "spiritual man" was there; the "natural man" was there no longer.

In the light of this word even the most unspiritual mind cannot fail in some degree of sympathy with St. Paul's enthusiasm in his work, or to understand the ecstasy with which he regarded the person of his Lord, or to know what he meant when he said that his "conversation," his daily life, was lived in heaven. The spiritual, so far as this, takes the look of the natural.

When we open his epistles and read them from this point of view, with this word as their key, they all—no matter what their occasion or what themes they passingly treat—take the character of the summons to the Metanoia. Back to this, in some form, they always come. He rings, as we said, endless changes upon the word. The thought of it appears in innumerable forms of expression. It would be one prolonged and many-sided illustration of the idea if we were to quote from him as profusely as we would like. But our space will permit only a selection of a few passages where the most direct reference is made, and where the "noëtic faculty" is also implied.

He said to the Romans: "Be not con-

The Metanoia of St. Paul.

formed to this world: but be ye Transformed by the Renewing of the Mind [μεταμορφοῦσθε τῇ, ανακαινώσαι τοῦ νοός, Rom. xii. 2]."

He said to the Corinthians: "We have the Mind [νοῦν] of Christ (1 Cor. ii. 16). . . . We all . . . are Transformed into the same image from glory to glory, even as by the Spirit of the Lord (2 Cor. iii. 18). . . . If any man be in Christ, he is a New Creature: old things are passed away; behold, all things are become New" (2 Cor. v. 17).

He said to the Ephesians: "That . . . God. . . . may give unto you a spirit of Wisdom [σοφίας] and Revelation in the Knowledge [ἐπιγνώσει] of Him [Christ]: the eyes of your heart being Enlightened; that ye may know," etc. (Eph. i. 17, 18); "Henceforth walk not as the Gentiles also walk, in the vanity of their Mind [νοὸς], having the Understanding [τῇ διανοίᾳ] darkened, being alienated from the life of God through the Ignorance [ἄγνοιαν] that is in them. . . . But ye have not so Learned Christ; if so be that ye have heard Him, and have been Taught in Him, even as Truth is in Jesus: that ye put off concerning the former manner of life, the old man; . . . and be Renewed in the spirit of your Mind [νοὸς]; and that ye put on the New Man" (Eph. iv. 18–24).

He said to the Colossians: " Seeing that ye have put off the old man with his deeds; and have put on the New Man, which is Renewed in Knowledge after the image of Him that created him " (Col. iii. 9, 10).

He said to Timothy: "The servant of the Lord must . . . be . . . apt to Teach, patient; in meekness instructing those that oppose themselves; if God peradventure will give them Metanoia unto Knowledge [εἰς ἐπίγνωσιν] of the Truth " (2 Tim. ii. 24, 25).

But we must now pass on to an occasion in which he used the word itself, and by force of circumstances less in a spiritual than in an intellectual and popular sense.

When he confronted the Stoics and Epicureans in the Areopagus, roused to indignation by the evidences of image-worship around him, and to quick perception of the opportunity offered him by an altar to an Unknown God—to him so near in association with the Unnamed God of his own people, but to them only, at the most, a philosophical dream—when, in coming before such an audience, he had to burn his Hebrew ships, for he could beat no retreat upon the traditions of his own religion, quote no Scriptures but those of their own poets, and reason with them only upon their own premises; when, if he spoke at all, he must speak to the intellect, and to an intellect which would care very little for an appeal to the heart, and not even understand an allusion to "sin" as a moral alienation; when all his tact and ingenuity were exerted to get uninterrupted to the "new thing" they desired to hear and he wished to announce; when he had stated the nature of the one living and true God in a way to command their respect, and in a way to enlarge their conception of Him who should remain no longer "Unknown," if he could reveal Him to their understanding—what did he say? "The times of Ignorance therefore God overlooked; but now he commandeth men that they should all everywhere Change their Mind [Μετανοεῖν];" namely, unto the Knowledge of One who was to "judge the world in righteousness."

Without question St. Paul spoke as near as he could to the sense of classic Greek under such Attic circumstances, and we are not justified in here interpreting the word in any other way. He could not have expected them to put the full construction upon it which lay in his own mind, and with which it must have vaguely rung in their ears as it came forth with the tone of his own intense consciousness. All that they could have understood was an appeal to "change their views"; to come to a conception of the Divine Nature more worthy of those who were "the offspring of God"; to accept this great "knowledge" which he now communicated in place of the "ignorance" which their altar confessed. The very most that their usage could admit into the word he had employed was an ethical import, sometimes, though rarely, attached to it; but it must have been in this instance very dimly discerned, if at all. If there was anything like "regret" to be felt, it was, most probably, only displeasure with themselves that they should have been so mistaken. Certainly nothing so strong as *penitence* could have been dreamed of by St. Paul. He was intent upon something beyond, to which the intellectual impression or emotion he had created would be a stepping-stone, namely, "the Man whom God had

The Metanoia of St. Paul.

ordained "—the Christ. For this, and up to this, he would "Change their Mind."[1]

How utterly inconceivable, at any rate, is a call to *repentance*, as it is translated in our version, both the Old and the New, in the connection of such an attempt to commend the revelation he proclaimed to the confidence and respect of these speculative men!

We must leave to the reader the further examination of passages in the New Testament where "Metánoia" in some form appears, and is still rendered "*repentance*" in the New Version. Here they all are in a foot-note, and he can judge for himself whether, in every case (and in some cases most expressly), a more distinct reference to the *Changed Mind*, in the profound sense we have given the phrase, would not be an improvement upon the more emotional and less fruitful idea suggested by the word "*repentance*." It will be found used, in many of these instances, not in a general, but in a

---

[1] There is an appositeness between the inscription ΑΓΝΩΣΤΩ ΘΕΩ in the beginning of the speech, and the expressions ἀγνοίας and μετανοεῖν at the end, which is very significant.

special application, when its great meaning is curdled, as it were, into the expression of a single feeling repellent of sin under the *revelation of righteousness;* when thought, perception, knowledge, conscience, penitence, and the will are combined into such a strong revolt of the entire man from an evil course as to change the character of his life. A rendering which keeps any of these powerful and necessary elements out of sight is more than an unfortunate one.[1]

[1] According to the text of Westcott and Hort. This text has been followed elsewhere in this edition of the essay when there has been a departure from the Authorized Version.

Μετανοέω: Matt. iii. 2, iv. 17, xi. 20, 21, xii. 41; Mark i. 15, vi. 12; Luke x. 13, xi. 32, xiii. 3, 5, xv. 7, 10, xvi. 30, xvii. 3, 4; Acts ii. 38, iii. 19, viii. 22, xvii. 30, xxvi. 20; 2 Cor. xii. 21; Rev. ii. 5 (twice), 16, 21 (twice), 22, iii. 3, 19, ix. 20, 21, xvi. 9, 11.

Μετάνοια: Matt. iii. 8, 11; Mark i. 4; Luke iii. 3, 8, v. 32, xv. 7, xxiv. 47; Acts v. 31, xi. 18, xiii. 24, xix. 4, xx. 21, xxvi. 20; Rom. ii. 4; 2 Cor. vii. 9, 10; 2 Tim. ii. 25; Heb. vi. 1, 6, xii. 17; 2 Pet. iii. 9.

VII.

METANOIA THE WORD OF CHRIST TO THE PRESENT AGE.

IN all that we have now said we have shown ourselves anxious that, in the translated New Testament, the Summons in the original proclamation of the Gospel should be made to appear as profound and significant as it really was, and thus be made to unite itself with the intellectual and spiritual life of the present century as keenly as it did with the first. We would have it a fresh, living, all-comprehensive, all-powerful Summons now.

We desire this, first, in order that the unity of the New Testament may be seen to lie in it from the beginning as in a germ, and to branch and flower from it in every part, as from a stem.

We desire this, next, for the more important and vital reason that the ethical and practical character of the religion of Christ may be revealed in its real supremacy over the emotional theory which has so long disproportionately prevailed.

But, above all, we desire it—above all, from its including these and comprehending more—because it implies the use of *the entire nature of man*, intellectual, moral, affectional, spiritual, his human part and his divine part, in the act of apprehending and appropriating the truth of God. The whole *Noûs* is appealed to, the whole Mind is engaged in seeing Him who is invisible, and in doing His will.

For it is now the unhappy fact that the Christian religion is so specifically applied to one portion of this Mind and to one state of it that if the requisition were strictly insisted upon as a standard and test, many persons of the purest character and highest principle would be denied the name of Christian, though palpably actuated by the faith and spirit of Christ. The *penitential* condition is not all, however much it may be. The recognition of Christ may spring from a wider surface and even a deeper principle than that one agonized nerve in the retina of the soul.

"METANOEĪTE!" It is a generous word, looking outwardly from the life that now is to that which is to come. Let us have its equivalent in gospel and epistle wherever it appears. Let it speak to *this* age, at least, in full, not muffled, articulation—to this age with its wide speculation upon the mystery of being, with its agnostic revolt from the religion that is preached, with its critical study of the historic Christ, and yet latent disposition to believe in Him.

"Metanoeīte!" It is time that the Herald uttered it again as He uttered it once. It bears to us the all-necessary message of contradiction and the all-necessary announcement of a revolution. It brings with it the true and everlasting tidings—always *news* to blind and mortal men—that the apparent conditions of this life are the illusion of flesh and sense, and that the real conditions of life are the very reverse of what we are prone to think and believe. The Eternal and the Spiritual are all; the temporal and the material are but the shadows of that substance.

The Great Meaning of Metánoia.

It were a bold word from any but a divine mouth, we should say, and yet the human tongue has been uttering it, virtually, all along in another sphere. What has been the proclamation of Science in her own material world but "Metanoeīte! Change your Mind from the near testimony of Sense to the distant witness of Discovery":

Sense says, "The sun rises in the east and revolves about the earth; the earth is the centre of the celestial sphere." But Science—Knowledge—proclaims a contradiction, and, with it, a revolution: "It is the earth that goes round the sun; the sun is but one of that starry host; the blue firmament melts into illimitable space; it is an illuminated universe that lies out there, in which this apparently ponderous globe floats like an atom in a sunbeam."

So Science, an echo of the divine voice, has enlarged, reversed, the whole consciousness of man. Her Metanoia has been proclaimed not only here, but everywhere in her material field. Whithersoever she has gone, nature has inverted its apparent order, its phenomena have widened out into principles that were once unknown, and the first human impression of them has had to be revoked.

It is an image, a parallel, of the Christian faith. The whole universe of the Spiritual is likewise being revealed to the knowledge of mankind. Time is declared to be of Eternal moment, and death the fullness of Life. We may discern the character of that other sphere by its inverse relation, point for point, to this.

Given, then, we say, the intellectual realization of this to men, their moral consciousness will rise to it, their spiritual nature will enlarge with it, their hearts and their lives will deepen to the measure of it. They will revolt more and more from sin and from the world.

This is *conversion* indeed; this is the Birth from Above.

We can now imagine how, under such a conception, the pulpit would awake to the grandeur of its work, how the Church would awake to the grandeur of her cause. The themes of the one, the methods of the other, would move with splendor and with power to one definite and mighty end: the Summon-

The Great Meaning of Metánoia.

ing of mankind to the Metanoia, this New Mind, and the announcement of *everything* on the divine side of life which would inspire and create it.

For we are just on the verge of a great epoch. All this intellectual activity in the material world is surely working towards a moment of reaction when the same intensity of movement will turn the other way, and the universal demand will be for a knowledge of the Spiritual. The voice of material Science, crying in the wilderness, will be found to have been preparing the way for this. It will turn out to have been uttering a word which has roused the "expectation" of this age. Out of all this agnostic dust and ashes shall mount again the cry, "Metanoeīte! for the Kingdom of Heaven is at hand."

Let us see to it that neither the Bible, the Church, nor the pulpit gives, in that great revealing day, an uncertain sound.

But our space is exhausted; yet one word more to carry our theme to its most practical and highest point.

We have said all when we say that "Metanoia" and "Revelation" are correlative terms, one always implying the other. As large, therefore, as we understand the Revelation to be, we must understand the Metanoia to be. They are reciprocal, as they develop, in character and degree.

In their meeting and blending within us, then, we become partakers of the Divine Nature and are saved. What begins with being a "Change of Mind toward God" deepens and broadens, as our nature turns all its disk that way, into that supreme reflection of God in the soul, "*faith* in our Lord Jesus Christ."

Faith is the Metanoia touched to the quick. Faith is the Metanoia when it has reached the vital fibers of our being; "the substance of things hoped for, the evidence of things not seen"; "God, who commanded the light to shine out of darkness, shining into our hearts, to give the light of the Knowledge of the glory of God in the face of Jesus Christ."

So it is the Metanoia which is bearing us heavenwards in Him. "We are Transformed into the same image from glory to glory." "We were sometime darkness, but now are we light in the Lord." "We press toward the mark for the prize of the Upward Calling of

God in Christ Jesus." More and more is the earthly nature dissolving away and releasing the heavenly one; deeper and deeper is the transfiguration working within; and it will not cease even when we have passed the gates of death, and

> " Heaven opens on our eyes; our ears
> With sounds seraphic ring!"

What will be the inburst of another world upon the soul but the Change of Changes, the supreme Metanoia of the Eternal Life!

THE VIEW OF MATTHEW ARNOLD.

WE are glad to add the testimony of still another independent scholar to the primary potency of the great Greek expression which opens the New Testament.

This time the claim for it is entirely ethical; the noëtic element is not foremost, but follows an inward awakening of the moral consciousness, although *that* is first brought about by perception and thought. This striking conception of the word comes from Matthew Arnold, an equal master in Greek with De Quincey, gifted with the same philosophic and theological insight, and a great Biblical student besides. In the case of De Quincey the view was a passing burst of inspiration over the word, and he makes no more of it. In the case of Arnold it comes in—though also quite episodically—as a part of a profound study into the genius of Christianity as it arose in Israel under the teaching of Christ. But he has an especial point to make—a protest against the subsequent metaphysical and dogmatic perversion of the original Semitic simplicity of Christian truth, the product of what he calls the "Aryan genius"—and it therefore does not fall in with his plan to make as much as he might have done either of the intellectual or the spiritual evolution of the principle so fully embodied, as we believe, in the expression. The

The Great Meaning of Metánoia.

working of both is strongly suggested, but, it seems to us, the vital and causative connection between what he calls the "method" of Jesus—i.e., Metanoia—and what he calls His "secret"—the utter renunciation of the lower self which culminated in "the word of the cross"—is not as vividly drawn out as it might have been.

But the point of interest now is his passing allusion to our word. In putting it here in connection with that of De Quincey we show not only the magnificent sweep of its meaning, from the ethical to the intellectual and back, but how completely the idea of *repentance* is thrown out of all association with it by two great scholars and thinkers whose imaginations had not been discolored by any theological prepossession and tradition, and who, as born and bred English churchmen, knew exactly what "*repentance*" was understood theologically to mean. The following passages are from "Literature and Dogma":

"To have the *thoughts* in order as to certain matters was *conduct*. This was the 'method' of Jesus: *setting up a great unceasing inward movement of attention and verification in matters which are three fourths of human life (righteousness), where to see true and to verify is not difficult.* . . . Watch carefully what passes *within you*, that you may obey the voice of conscience. . . . This, we say, is the 'method' of Jesus. To it belongs His use of that important word which in the Greek is Metánoia. We translate it '*repentance*,' a mourning and lamenting over our sins; and we translate it wrong. Of 'Metánoia,' as Jesus used the word, the *lamenting one's sins was a* small part; the main part was something far more active and fruitful, the setting up an immense new inward movement for obtaining the rule of life. And ' Metánoia,' accordingly, is *a change of the inner man.*

" Mention and recommendation of this inwardness there often was, we know, in prophet or psalmist; but to make mention of it was one thing, to *erect it into a positive method* was another. Christianity has made it so familiar that to give any freshness to one's words about it is now not easy; but to its first recipients it was abundantly fresh and novel. It was the introduction, in morals and religion, of the famous *Know thyself* of the Greeks; and this among a people deeply serious, but also wedded to moral and religious routine, and singularly devoid of flexibility and play of mind. For them it was a revolution. . . . This is the true line of religion; it was the line of Jesus. To work the renovation needed He *concentrated His efforts upon a method of inwardness,* of taking counsel of *conscience.*" (Page 174.)

"Christ's new and different way of putting things was the secret of His succeeding where the prophets could not. . . . *He put things in such a way that His hearers were led to take each rule or fact of conduct by its inward side, its effect upon the heart and character; then the reason of the thing, the meaning of what had been mere matter of blind rule, flashed upon them.* . . . The hardest rule of conduct came to appear to them infinitely reasonable and natural, and therefore infinitely prepossessing." (Page 94.)

" While the Old Testament says, ' Attend to conduct,' the New Testament says, ' Attend to the feelings and dispositions whence conduct proceeds!' And as attending to conduct had very much degenerated into deadness and formality, attending to the *springs of conduct* was a revelation, a *revival of intuitive and fresh perceptions*, a touching of morals with emotion. . . . Man came under a new dispensation, and made with God a second covenant." (Page 96.)

"At the Christian era . . . the time had come *for inwardness* and *self-construction*—a time to last till the self-construction is fully achieved." (Page 101.)

It will be noticed that while De Quincey, taking the summons "Metanoeïte" as a word to the whole world in all ages, gives rein to the whole intellectual consciousness, Arnold keeps it within its original bounds as addressed peculiarly to Israel, and addressed not so much at first to the intellect of Israel as—through a wondrous tact in teaching—to the latent spiritual consciousness, the intellect then awakening to the rationale of the law. But this double witness of opposite minds from opposite directions to the same philological profundity in the word is very impressive.

THE ECLIPSE OF METÁNOIA BY PŒNITENTIA.

I.

AN IMPOSSIBLE EXPEDIENT TO END IT: "RE-PENTANCE" TO BE MADE TO MEAN METANOIA.

THE suggestion of the theme of this Additional Essay came about in the following way:

During a recent residence in London we saw a notice in an American Church paper of a kind reference to the essay on Metánoia, by Dr. Brooke Foss Westcott, which seemed to indicate an agreement with the view we had taken. As Dr. Westcott (now the Bishop of Durham, but at the time Canon of Westminster, and Regius Professor of Divinity, Cambridge) had been one of the most distinguished and influential of the scholars engaged upon the revision of the New Testament, and had been especially prominent in furnishing the Greek text which formed the groundwork of the New Version, we had reason to suppose that the reference might be accompanied with some allusion to the action of the revisers on the rendering of Μετάνοια. But even aside from that, we felt that any expression of assent, however qualified, in coming from such an authority, would carry with it a weight and a consequence that would command the highest respect.

A note of inquiry elicited this courteous reply:

"6 SCROPE TERRACE,
"CAMBRIDGE, November 19, 1887.

"There was a reference to your essay in a paper on the Revised Version, in the 'Expositor.' I have not a copy of the magazine at hand, but I think it was in the paper which appeared in August.

"I intended to say that you had brought out with singular power and truth the meaning of Μετάνοια, while I could not see that the translation could be modified.

"The preacher and the scholar must transfigure *repentance*, even as *fides* and *gratia* have been transfigured. In this work your essay will, I trust, be of eminent service."

The above extract gives all of the reply that refers to the essay, and is introduced here because it adds materially to the force of one of the remarks in the passage from the "Expositor," which will be found below.

This admirable statement, covering so briefly and yet so comprehensively the whole question, appears in one of a series of papers entitled "'Some Lessons of the Revised Version of the New Testament,' by Rev. Professor B. F. Westcott, D.D., D.C.L., Canon of Westminster" (August, 1887, p. 86).

As the passage is in the form of a foot-note, and bears no connection with anything in the text, it was apparently written in the proof after our essay had been read. The matter could hardly have suggested itself otherwise, as there had been no change in the translation of Μετάνοια, and therefore no occasion for discussion of the subject. The statement has an especial interest, therefore, not only as having been drawn out by the essay, but

The Eclipse of Metánoia by Pœnitentia.

also as conveying the mind of the revisers on the question of the rendering "*repentance*." If it does not explain their silence in passing over it, it suggests their difficulty in dealing with it. The passage is as follows:

"One most important group of words, rendered in the Authorized Version '*repent*,' '*repentance*' (μετανοεῖν, μετάνοια, μεταμέλεσθαι), offered great difficulties in translation.

"The first two Greek words (μετανοεῖν, μετάνοια) describe characteristically, in the language of the New Testament, a general change of mind, which becomes in its fullest development an intellectual and moral regeneration; the latter (μεταμέλεσθαι) expresses a special relation to the past, a feeling of regret for a particular action, which may be deepened into remorse.

"It was of paramount importance to keep one rendering for the former words, which are key-words of the gospel, and it was impossible to displace '*repent*,' '*repentance*,' which, though originally inadequate, are capable of receiving the full meaning of the original.

An Impossible Expedient to End It.

"No one satisfactory term could be found for μεταμέλεσθαι. In the passage where it occurs in the same context with μετάνοια it has been adequately rendered by 'regret' (2 Cor. vii. 8 ff.); and elsewhere the limited application of the feeling has been indicated by the reflexive rendering '*repent one's self*'—never '*repent*' absolutely (Matt. xxi. 29, 32, xxvii. 3; Heb. vii. 21); yet '*without repentance*' (ἀμεταμέλητος) (Rom. xi. 29) is unchanged.

"Dr. T. Walden has expounded the apostolic force of μετάνοια with great power and truth in an essay on 'The Great Meaning of the Word "Metánoia," Lost in the Old Version, Unrecovered in the New' (New York, 1882); but he has overlooked the fact that the idea of *repentance*, like that of μετάνοια itself, can be transfigured by Christian use, and that the force of words is not limited by their etymology."

II.

Μετάνοια TRANSFIGURED GREEK.

We are scarcely prepared to admit that we overlooked either of these points.

As to the first—"That the idea of *repentance*, like that of Μετάνοια itself, can be transfigured by Christian use."

The "idea of *repentance*," it seems to us, is so deeply lined in the word "*repentance*" that the physiognomy of the term is fixed beyond any power of essential alteration. Its intense look of sorrow may be and has been softened by Christian use into the expression of a pensive sense of unworthiness and guilt, and of a consequent mental determination which changes the character, the conduct, and the life; but the "fashion of its countenance" cannot be "altered" further than this, nor can its "raiment become white and dazzling," even as Μετάνοια was "transfigured" when it stood on the "high mountain apart" of the New Testament, and its "face did shine as the sun," and its "garments became white as the light."

The analogy suggested by the event which is so sacredly connected with the thought of "transfiguration" is here so true to the fact that we cannot but employ the force of the allusion.

Now every Christian idea was "described so characteristically in the language of the New Testament" that any word taken from common use to represent it was heightened even to heaven in its meaning.

And it was especially in the nature of a Greek word to bear such a transcendentalization. Indeed, we may be sure that the Greek was made the vehicle of the Gospel not only because it was historically so opportune, but because it was philologically so available; and no other of the three representative tongues that were heard around the cross could have uttered the message of the cross so well.

The Jew arraigned the Christ and the

Roman erected the cross; both were characteristically foremost on that ground; but to neither of them was intrusted "the word of the cross," which was to go into all lands and down to all ages.

The Jew was as dumb as Zacharias was when he tried to give the benediction. He had lost his prophetic faith, as he had lost his Old Testament tongue.

The Roman could only show "all the kingdoms of the world, and the glory of them." His language was their law, the regulating outcome of the same genius that had conquered them. It reflected the practical, material precision of his mind, but it was not, it never could be, except by infusion from without, elastic to the highest expression of spiritual ideas. It was not, it never could be, even under inspiration from above, equal to the adequate divine utterance of the truth whose "Kingdom was not of this world."

Most remarkable, most significant was it, then, that the commission to *reveal* that truth was laid upon the idealizing tongue of the Greek; while the commission to *order* the Kingdom, to give direction to its mechanism, and to give names to its appointments, was assumed by the methodizing tongue of the Roman.

Take now the words before us, Μετάνοια and *Repentance*, which Bishop Westcott associates under what we may understand as the metaphor of transfiguration. They are thoroughly representative. The one is the inaugurating word of the Greek New Testament, the other is the inaugurating word of its Latin translation; and in its Latin form (*Pœnitentia*) it is, according to the Latin mind, a precise equivalent of the Greek.

Μετάνοια is a word of classic origin and usage, but of extraordinary scriptural development. A process of transfiguration, after the sacred analogy we are thinking of, did actually take place in it. The change in our Lord, as described by the evangelists, was an outburst of inward radiance. Light did not fall *upon* Him. *It came from within Him.* It was His own—the latent effulgence in His human nature of His divine nature, prophetic of the glory that was about to be revealed in Him.

In like manner the first word used of Him, the first word used by Him, according to these evangelists, the word which opened His Kingdom when it was at hand, Μετάνοια, rose, through a like inward capacity for utterance, into a word of light-giving power. It was "transfigured" indeed. It turned out to be an anticipation, in a single compressed expression, of the whole rationale of Christianity as that new faith was afterwards unfolded in the New Testament. It held the whole idea and method of the coming revelation in germ. It contained the principle which made the religion of Christ absolutely original—the principle of the radical renewal of the nature of man under the working of a Knowledge revealed to him from above, under the operation of a Spirit which came to him from above; through which Knowledge and through which Spirit his nature was set free to do spontaneously, and not by legal regulation, all that it ought to do: "his flesh being subdued to the spirit," "sin could have no dominion over him: for he was not under law, but under grace." "There was therefore now no condemnation to them that were in Christ Jesus. For the law of the Spirit of Life in Christ Jesus made men free from the law of sin and death."

Metánoia Transfigured Greek.

Hence Μετάνοια was the "key-word of the Gospel," as Bishop Westcott finely says. It opened to and potentially entered into everything. No door called by any other name, such as "faith," no chamber known by any other name, such as "renewal," was beyond the application of this master key.

Turn now to the expression which has undertaken to supply its place both in the proclamation and in the operation of the Kingdom of God.

"*Repentance*" is a word of classical Latin origin and of Latin theological and ecclesiastical descent. The core of it is not *mind*, but *pain*. The note of it is not of emancipation, but of condemnation. The scope of it is not spiritual, but juridical. The working of it is not joyful, but sorrowful. Its face is turned in horror towards sin, not in rapture towards righteousness. It is a way to righteousness, but by the way of retreat. It flees the evil in fear of "penalty"—of the punitive action of God or of its own conscience. In its effective operation it can take hold of the Mind, change the mental attitude, determine the mental purpose, but it can never alone renew the whole spiritual constitution of the Mind. It may be the beginning of amendment of life, but is not potential to the consummation of life. It is retrospective, and it leads to introspection, often to intense spiritual self-consciousness, often to the most humble gratitude to God for salvation through Christ. In the awakening of Μετάνοια it is always at hand, a powerful phase of it, an inevitable incident of it, a helpful, if not encouraging, attendant upon it.

The Latin instinct amounted to insight when it made so much of *pœnitentia* as an element of Μετάνοια, but the instinct overshot the insight when in aiming at the one it lost sight of the other. All Christians have adopted the excellent word, because, so far as it goes, it is a true word; and the above, we believe, is an accurate account of its theological acceptation among us.

But can it be "transfigured," even till it is as radiant as the word which illumined the face of Christ in the beginning, and illumined all His teaching and the teaching of His apostles to the end? Has it any interior capacity to develop such a new transformation? On the contrary, will it not prove utterly intractable under such a strain against its grain? We can imagine it disguised, but never transfigured. We can imagine it glowing as with phosphorus, but never with genuine light. We can imagine it raised to such a power by a sort of conjuration, but what a mere apparition it would be! Who of us can conceive of a word so intrinsically dark ever passing itself off as conveying a conception so bright and so noble as this:—"a *general* Change of Mind, which becomes in its fullest development an *intellectual and moral Regeneration*"?

III.

"REPENTANCE" PERSISTENT LATIN.

LET us now turn to the other point which we are also hardly ready to admit that we overlooked—"that the force of words is not limited by their etymology."

This is said, of course, in the interest of the idea that "*repentance*" can be made to express the meaning of Μετάνοια by ignoring the origin and usage of the Latin-English word.

If now, we follow out the line of this suggestion, we shall be led into a more positive exposure of its claims.

Our language is full of words which once possessed a signification that is now extinct, and which have since taken up an unlimited range of application because of their independence of all etymology. Our dictionaries are overrun with such hermit-crabs, occupy-

"Repentance" Persistent Latin.

ing and dragging about the shells of words whose primary meanings have long ago outgrown or abandoned them. But *pœnitentia* has never been one of this sort. It has never exhibited any such facility in, or even any tendency to, shedding its shell. On the contrary, its whole history shows that it has been endowed with an extraordinary determination to hold on to its original meaning, and as extraordinary a capacity to accommodate itself to all circumstances, *without forgetting the idea out of which it was made and the end unto which it was appointed.* If there ever was a word which has been as phenomenal for persistency in preserving its type, in both outer form and inner life, as other words have been phenomenal for the curious results of a willing variation from what they once were, it is this very word, which we know so well in its English expression as "*repentance.*"

It resembles, as we recall its long career, that famous species of the nautilus which, from the outset, seems to be endowed with an instinct of predestination. The creature simply enlarges itself under the necessity of development that is upon it, without abandoning anything that ever essentially belonged to it. As it outgrows its quarters it builds on one chamber after another to accommodate the expanding eras of its life. As it increases externally it is always the same, coiling closely about its original axis. As it develops internally it is again always the same, clinging as closely to the seat of its original vitality, even keeping open communication, through the whole series of its dividing partitions, by a living siphuncular cord, with the cell in which it began.

Pœnitentia, in like manner, has ever exhibited a similar potency in enlarging the scope of its own application in just such a succession of chambers, and in developing just such an unchangeable purpose to mean exactly, and no more, what it was primarily intended to mean. You may look into its black mouth, and there is the self-same primitive cephalopod, still sufficient unto itself because occupying the sufficient mouthpiece of an idea which comes home to all ages and to all conditions of mankind.

It comes so universally home because its origin was so primitively homely. Its whole meaning arose in and was represented by the Sanskrit monosyllable PÛ,—*to cleanse from dirt*. *Pœnitentia* has always retained and has always sustained this primary idea of *purgation*. Its career has been marked by progressive historic stages, in every one of which this idea has in some way prevailed.

When it developed itself among the primeval Greeks, it was ποινή, a word for blood-money. A murderer, say, by a redeeming payment, *purged* himself of all further responsibility to the relatives of the man he had slain. Their vengeance was satisfied; they no longer pursued him. Hence the word came to signify "vengeance."

When the idea developed itself among the Latins it was *pœna;* and it rose with Roman civilization into an expression closely identified with the criminal law. It became a designation for all grades of *punishment* inflicted under the law, whereby those who had offended or injured the community made their peace with it, satisfied justice—in a word, *purged* themselves—by bearing the penalty which had been fixed upon as measuring the degree of their transgression. To use another word from the same root, they *expiated* their crime against the state. To use still another, they were *purified* in the eye of the law by what they had suffered.

The term *pœna* thus belonged to the court of law and to the language of the judgment-seat. Whence our modern duplication of it in the legal phrase "pain and penalty."

But the expression *pœnitentia*, which was formed out of it, and which represented the *pain* of one who thus bore the *penalty* of his misdeeds, was never a legal term. The law in that day did not concern itself with what the condemned criminal felt. But the popular mind did, and put itself in sentimental sympathy with him. Hence came the coining of *pœnitentia*, as a current word in Latin literature for the sorrow or regret which followed when one had made a mistake or committed an error of any kind. It meant exactly the *after-care* which was conveyed by Μεταμέλεια (Metaméleia) in the Greek. It was too variously used to retain any strong reminiscence of its origin. Indeed, its range of application came to be very much that of "*repentance*" in our common speech. It related to affairs or to morals, as the case might be, and indicated a feeling which might be fleeting and shallow or profound and effectual, according to the levity or gravity of the occasion.

When, however, *pœnitentia* was taken up by Latin Christianity it deepened into an expression of very serious import. It rapidly revived all the ideas and associations that lay in *pœna* itself. It put itself first on high moral ground exclusively. It put itself next on divine juridical ground exclusively. It seems to have met Μετάνοια near the close of the second century, when Christian ideas were beginning to find utterance in the Latin tongue. Up to that moment the universal church, even in Rome itself, spoke but one language—the language of the New Testament. But now the "Old Latin" version arose in North Africa, and the Latin lawyer Tertullian began to write.

The springs which hitherto had burst from the hills were now made to send their living waters through a Roman aqueduct. Practical and available precision of idea set in. The Latin version began to mould the theology of the age.

It is quite evident that Μετάνοια was already in a condition to meet the new movement half-way. It had degenerated from its New Testament use. It had subsided from its apostolic height. We have neither time nor space for reasons and conjectures why, as they suggest themselves in contemplating a period of which we know very little, except that there was a general declension after the Apostolic Age. But it would seem as if Μετάνοια had already lost its etymology, and now drew its signification from the idea of μετά and ἄνοια, a return from madness or folly. We know at least this much: that Lactantius, a century later, so understood and interpreted it, giving his impression of its import in the rendering *resipiscentia*, a word which Beza afterwards worked for what it was worth, in his avoidance of the Romish *pœnitentia* of the Vulgate. But at the time we are speaking of, Μετάνοια, now possibly no higher than Metaméleia, appears to have assimilated itself very kindly with *pœnitentia*, which, accordingly, with Roman promptitude and energy, at once undertook to dominate and direct the thought of the Church.

After this a sad fate awaited Μετάνοια itself. Having thus sunk its apostolic identity, its degeneration went on in the usage of Greek ecclesiastical speech, till finally it sank so low as to stand only for a minor *penitential* genuflection; so many "metanoias"—say, bowings of the head—for such and such a peccadillo!

Strangely and curiously enough, too, the original New Testament idea of it was only finally saved by the symbol with which it had been scripturally coupled, βάπτισμα Μετανοίας.[1] "Baptism," a word adopted letter for letter by the Latin from the Greek, but coupled in the Latin version with *pœni-*

---

[1] It is very clear to us that the "Báptisma" of John, as twinned with his "Metánoia," was a symbol of *revivification*—an intimation of it as it was afterwards apostolically understood. The idea of water as a symbol of cleansing was obvious, commonplace, and universal. But this rite was, in the whole tremendous manner of it, an invocation of the power of water in a way that was as profound, peculiar, and original as Christianity itself. It pointed expressly to the work of the Spirit, which was not to purify but to re-create. And it pointed as expressively to the work of water as the renewer and restorer of life. We can only hint at this its suggestive coincidence with the meaning of Metánoia. The view can be impressively substantiated, but not now, and here.

tentia, in the sense of "purification," had in itself strength enough to keep alive in theological thought its primitive and only true association with "regeneration."

IV.

THE ROMAN UTILIZATION OF "REPENTANCE."

But to come back to our main point. Let us follow very briefly, yet, we hope, sufficiently, the adventures of our nautilus *pœnitentia*.

Tertullian tells us in the opening of his "*De Pœnitentia*" that all former general literary notions of it must be dismissed; that as a Christian word it meant "a passion of the mind, or grief for the offense of our former acts." This exclusive exaltation of it arose from the consciousness of *sin in the sight of God*, and from its consequent emotion, which was more a terror of His judgments than a delight in His glad tidings. Under the fear of Him and the flight from evil the life was changed. The sinner, awakening to the madness of his course, took shelter in the Christian community as in a city of refuge, and there, in that centre of light, his soul became irradiated with the joy of faith, the consciousness also of having been redeemed, and hence of absolute security in the household which gathered around the table of the Lord.

But in the practical working of that community of grateful love in the saving presence of Christ, the sinful propensities of human nature proved too irrepressible; the theoretical horror, also, of evil in that age of speculation over it, in addition to this practical experience with it, proved too intense; and the juridical tradition of the Old Testament, besides, was felt to be too authoritative (the New Testament had scarcely been put together yet), for the idea of *pœnitentia* to remain in its single and simple form. The Roman genius for law and practical organization, therefore, soon laid hold of it, and began to develop all its resources from that time on.

The word began by meeting admirably, because after a legal manner, a difficulty which had developed itself in the Christian community from the very beginning. We find it spoken of as so applied in the latter part of Tertullian's treatise. He speaks of those who had turned out derelict to the faith and delinquent to its righteousness, and who had therefore brought reproach upon the community. The Church had to vindicate its own purity before the world, and yet, unlike the State under similar circumstances, it had to sympathize in mercy with the sinner. So *pœnitentia* now came before it not only, as at first, with the signification of tears unto turning, but of tears unto returning; not only "primary *repentance*," but "secondary *repentance*," as Tertullian terms it. Under the strange and pathetic phenomenon of the excommunicated—the *penitents*, as they came to be called—praying for restoration, a condition of things daily increasing in intensity and becoming a fixed feature in the Church, the word soon concentrated most of its force upon the latter meaning. It developed a growing legal aspect as it elaborated itself in dealing both justly and mercifully with the crowd of *penitents* which thronged about the church doors and even groveled at the feet of the presbyters, pleading for readmission. There they were, making their appeal in every possible way, trying to *purge* themselves by voluntary austerities, to *expiate* their offense by self-punishments, and to make *satisfaction* to the authorities by such outward demonstrations of sorrow as would prove their sincerity. And all the Church could do was to cry, as it now supposed John the Baptist to have cried, "*Pœnitentiam agite!*" "*Do penance!*" and to set about reducing the business of restoration to a system, the contrivance of various tests and conditions under which it could, with safety to itself and a good conscience towards God, "remit" the sin and readmit the sinner.

Then began a question and controversy, which lasted for many generations, over the extent of the Church's authority to legislate against sin, and to occupy the judgment-seat, and to administer the prerogative of God in "pardoning" or "absolving."

It was a blind work that it had undertaken, for it could not see into the heart; it could only judge by the outside; and it could only exact coarse external evidences of reformation. The whole realm of the inward mind and of the inner motives was out of its province; and therefore just so much of the Kingdom of God as was "within" and that came not "with observation" was beyond its jurisdiction.

The Roman Utilization of "Repentance."

Nevertheless the Roman genius rose to the occasion, and did not hesitate to construct the scales of divine justice with greater and greater ingenuity of elaboration, and with fitter and fitter adaptation to its own ready handling.

It were needless to follow our nautilus *pœnitentia* as it went on from epoch to epoch, camerating itself around one crisis after another, and evolving a whole system of expiatory penalties, until it culminated finally in the "Sacrament of Penance," a grand purgative transaction under hierarchical administration, with a jurisdiction extending, on the one hand, into Purgatory for the dead, and, on the other, into the equally questionable realm of Casuistry for the living.

However, it looked at last as if the Latin creature had expended all its vitality and was about to turn into death and corruption, when it reached the climax of its assumption in the sale of indulgences, and the consequent reaction of the Reformation burst upon Christendom. One would suppose that the word would have perished in Protestantism after it had led the Church up to such a scandalous catastrophe as the loss of its hierarchical hold on the conscience and the future destiny of mankind. But no. The Reformation turned out to be only the reconstruction of another chamber. The inexhaustible energy and persistency of a word which had so powerful an etymology, and a usage in idea which had all along been nourished by the Vulgate, now came forth in a new manifestation. Instead of drawing back into its shell and dying there, *pœnitentia* magnified itself the more. It began to secrete for itself a more roomy and refined compartment. Under the influence of the Vulgate it rose anew in almost every European version of the New Testament; and in no version, though direct from the Greek, did Μετάνοια in its high apostolic meaning find room enough to breathe. The Latin substitute remained in all its primeval force, still keeping up its suction from its Aryan origin in the idea of purgation, only dropping its coarse medieval accretions; and so around it gathered again the fabric of the modern popular theology, still Latin to the core.

V.

THE GOSPEL IN THE SHADOW OF THE LAW.

IN the facile English tongue the Latin cephalopod *pœnitentia* put forth three tentacles under which English Christianity entered upon its practical conception of the Gospel. All three may now be found in the English Prayer-book—happily only two of them in the American: "*penance*," in the sense of discipline; "*penitence*," in the sense of contrition; and "*repentance*" or "*re-penitence*," in the sense of such an effectual working of either or of both as resulted in amendment of life.

As "*repentance*," therefore, it took the foremost place, and as "*repentance*," though often badly confounded with the other two, it was now expounded as identical in meaning with Μετάνοια, dragging back the Greek idea into its own limitations, and so attenuating the substance of the Greek word as finally to put its ideal quality out of sight altogether. Μετάνοια was again Latinized out of its very soul, and its essence shrank away into a circumstance.

A scholar and theologian like Jeremy Taylor (who wrote his great treatise on *"Repentance"* about forty years after 1611, in order to correct the false impressions which were inevitable to the word), might do his best to fix and distinguish the lost meaning, and to assemble under the term *"repentance"* the ideas of "faith" and "renewal" and "reconciliation," but the word was not to be so easily rarified out of its concrete force. With all his ingenuity it baffled and contradicted him. He could not make it "serve his turn," as he said it would.

And so it will always stand for what it originally was, and so it will always reverse the theory and the action of the Gospel. Its misleading tendency can never be expounded out of it. It will always give the Gospel a legal aspect; it will always, therefore, dim the near Fatherhood of God in setting Him upon a distant judgment-seat; it will always put

Christ in a wrong relation to both God and man; it will always proclaim that man must be purged from sin by his own self-condemnation and by his formal discharge from a Divine Tribunal, and not set free (ἄφεσις), first and essentially, through that renewal of his nature (Μετάνοια) under the knowledge of God in Christ and the inspiration of the Spirit, by which only the strength of sin is undermined and the creative work of God in the soul resumed.

It is useless, also, to deny or ignore the fact of this perversion and reversal of the ideally sublime and gracious message of the good tidings of great joy, in the presence of the forbidding systems of theology, partly inherited from Latin sources, partly constructed by modern ingenuity, which have been nurtured and sustained, as well as, to a degree, originally inspired, by this Latin conception of *pœnitentia*. With the undying legalism which is imbedded in it; with its undying reminiscence of vengeance, of punishment, of expiation; with its undying suggestion that the Change of Mind is only a change of will wrought by fear; with its undying determination towards a theory of radical corruption in which tears are an all-powerful cleansing agent; with its too ready readaptation, therefore, of the method in which human nature was dealt with in the Old Testament—as itself a creature of the law, whether Mosaic or Roman—it has erected a judgment-seat in the heavens and earth, and put upon the face of God the frown of outraged justice, and lowered the great and graphic metaphor which pervades the New Testament —simply for convenience and vividness of expression in an age and to a people penetrated with legal ideas—into an actual divine reality; pressing the pervading parable literally, as corresponding point for point to the forensic and judicial arrangements which have come up in communities of men when dealing with evil.

Even thus, as we conceive, has this court-room conception of Christianity been made its working theory, ever since the *penitential* idea was given this initial and commanding position in the New Testament and in the Church.

"*Repentance*," when all its etymological potency is challenged and drawn out by its use as a theological word, or rather as a dogmatic key-word—as it is when it is put in the place of Μετάνοια—dominates the whole conception of the Gospel. It not only, as we say, reverses the order of its thought, and gives a wrong deflection to its ideas, but it infects everything within its reach.

It throws a shadow here and a color there even over the translation of the Greek Testament, and sustains the Latin tinge which pervades the texture of its English everywhere. It has thus obscured the absolute originality of the New Testament as compared with the Old. And it has thus facilitated the perpetuation of Judaism in the Church—that is, the dominance of externalism in taste and sentiment; of mechanism in methods of faith and devotion; of artificialism in thought and feeling; of literalism and conventionalism—all that is fatal to mental breadth and spiritual depth, all that shuts the universal humanity of Christ out of the universal heart.

And yet "*repentance*" is a word of indispensable value to us if it can be kept where it originally belonged in Latin literature, and where it really belongs now in common English speech; if it can be kept in the meaning it had in popular usage before its etymology was roused into activity by its adoption as a dogmatic principle, and before the call "*Repent ye!*" was understood to be the creative fiat of the new heavens and the new earth. We have to be grateful to the practical Latin genius for an expression which seizes upon all that poignancy of feeling with which the enlightened conscience turns against sin, and which describes with a dignity and depth given to no other word that sense of unworthiness and guiltiness which grows more and more acute as the standard of righteousness rises before every heart. In that, its true sphere, it is indeed a divine sequel to Μετάνοια, the shadow which witnesses to the power of that refulgent word. When we "turn from the darkness to the light"—which is the meaning of Μετάνοια—it is a remnant of the darkness, our individual, personal share of it, dogging our footsteps and keeping us humble amid all the glory that shines about us in the knowledge of Jesus Christ. May it always express the "Metaméleia" which it properly translates, and which Bishop Westcott defines so well to be "a special relation to the past; a feeling of regret for a particular action, which may be deepened into remorse," and —we may take the liberty of reminding him, with Scripture authority for it (see Matt. xxi. 29, where the son who refused to go to work "afterward *repented himself*, and went ")— deepened also into such a revulsion of feeling as brings with it amendment of conduct.

Most true is it, then, that, as Bishop Westcott says, "the force of words is not limited by their etymology;" but the remark cannot be applied, as he intends it to be applied, to "*repentance*," as an expression so plastic as to be easily moulded into the great meaning of Μετάνοια. The energy of its etymology is too monopolizing, too pervadingly positive, as all its history shows, when given a tempting occasion. It has been even powerful, aggressive, and intrusive enough to put the light of Μετάνοια under a bushel for ages, and no hopeful theory over the manipulation of words to suit our purpose ought to persuade us to trust it again.

VI.

"DISASTROUS TWILIGHT" IN THE REVISED VERSION.

WE are so careful in making a strong point of this because the revisers themselves were evidently influenced by a contrary impression when they decided not only to let the translation of Μετάνοια alone, but decided also to pass so quietly over it as not even to awaken a suspicion or a question as to its absolute equivalence. Indeed, Bishop Westcott would seem to be giving their view of the matter, and speaking on their behalf, when he says, "It was impossible to displace '*repent,*' '*repentance,*' which, though *originally inadequate, are capable of receiving the full meaning of the original.*"

This, it will be noticed, is his idea of the "transfiguration" of "*repentance*" put in a different way. It is an expression of confidence in the readiness of that Latin word to

"*Disastrous Twilight*" in the Revised Version.

take the stamp of the Greek word so thoroughly that its own original image would be obliterated, its own identity be lost. In default of the power to get rid of it, *it could be made to do.* All that he had just defined Μετάνοια to be—"an intellectual and moral regeneration"—all the "apostolic force" that we have claimed for Μετάνοια, which he admits to be a true exposition, is to be *put into it.* Its etymology is to be ignored. Its history is to be ignored. Even its everyday usage is to be ignored. It is to be arbitrarily understood to convey the "full meaning of the original" for which it has so long stood, and nevermore any meaning which it has all along had. It is only a Latin word with a Greek face. It spells "*repentance*," but it is to be pronounced "Metanoia."

What a curious spectacle would be presented if this could be done, and what a confession it would be of the impotence of our own tongue under the paralysis of a tradition! A word which was once thought to be a *translation*, but which has since turned out to be a perversion, going back into the original by a process of absorption, and henceforth depending upon the original for its definition! This would be putting the moon into the eye of the sun and expecting the sun to shine. Neither luminary would then give its appointed light. It would be an eclipse of the greater by the lesser: Μετάνοια turned into nought but a lurid ring, because of the ball of blackness at the centre of it.

It was to avoid the possibility of just such a "disastrous twilight" that, as Bishop Westcott says, "it was of paramount importance" to keep the word "*repentance*" clear and absolute in the version, unmixed with any association with its own former idea. In the version it should represent Μετάνοια, and Μετάνοια alone. Then the reader of the Revised Version, having discovered that "*repentance*" was a translation upwards into the meaning of Μετάνοια, would not be distracted from that conception of it, either by anything which "*repent*" might mean in popular speech, or by what it might mean elsewhere in the New Testament itself.

But out of this "paramount" necessity there arose a difficulty, as it turned out, which the revisers did not and could not successfully overcome. "*Repent*" had a double in the New Testament that would not down. There before them was Μεταμέλεσθαι ("Metamélesthai"), formidable and unremovable because of its rightful claim to both the physiognomy and the soul of the word "*repent*," as men generally use it on serious occasions. And Bishop Westcott is obliged to admit that in only one instance was it made to give way and go out of sight. Everywhere else it stood its ground, or rather its ground had to be yielded, because no other of its English kindred had weight and dignity enough to fill its place.

So the two luminaries of the Greek original—the one idea which rules the night of regret over things of the past, and figures so powerfully in the darkness of the Old Testament as the reflection of a sun as yet unrisen; and the other idea which rules the day of faith and righteousness, the sun that has since risen in the New—are represented in the Revised Version under conditions of most singular aberration and confusion. The lesser orb not only shines alone in its proper sphere six times out of seven, but also invades the day, even to hiding the very disk of the daylight, even to robbing it of its distinction as well as its function, even to making, through the mixture of the two, a ghastly monotone of all its twoscore and thirteen variants of light.

Such, then, is the result of the endeavor to cope with these two words in the original. *"Repentance"* has been given a heightened or intensified signification wherever it stands for Μετάνοια, and in its possession of this is to be its sole distinction. But *when and where* the distinction is to be made is left to the unlearned reader to find out for himself. In one part of the New Testament "*repent*" means one thing, and in another part another thing; and so, between these two stools of "*repentance*," he is still in as much danger as before the revision, of falling into that low conception of the apostolic idea which generally prevails.

Let us, now, however, draw from this mixture of the two words in the English Version a fair inference as to what " the *repentance* of the Gospel" is supposed to mean.

First, it is a retrospective act of the mind.

Second, it is a feeling specifically directed against sin.

Third, it is this in such intense action that it brings about a change in the conduct and life.

Fourth, it is this, also, in such effective action that it takes hold of the *mind;* so working upon the will as to change the mental habit and attitude, thus amounting to a conversion of the whole nature.

Fifth, and this mental and spiritual attitude *towards sin* is the full import of the word Μετάνοια.

Now the obvious thought that occurs to one is this: the whole of the above conception of "*repentance*" could have been easily put, by the New Testament writers, into the compass of Μεταμέλεια (" Metaméleia ")—which means " after-care." Why did they not do it? The expression would have lent itself most kindly to such a purpose. It could have been made to rise to any measure of that idea under their heightening hands. Besides that, Μεταμέλεια and Μετάνοια were often very near in signification, as employed in popular speech among the Greeks. They ran in close parallel on certain occasions—so much so that one would do as well as the other; though on other occasions they could diverge very widely apart. Why was Μεταμέλεια so carefully avoided, and Μετάνοια so conspicuously chosen? Because the idea of an *after-care* concentrated upon sin was not comprehensive enough. It did not take in the regenerative motive and principle. It did not suggest the illuminated condition and action of the whole Mind—Mind in the sense of Νοῦς—under which sin would lose its hold, would become less and less a dominating and deflecting thing, and faith become more and more a foremost and active instinct; under which the nerve would be more firm, the eye more fixed, in the aim at the mark, in the run for the goal. Hence, then came the selection and uniform employment of Μετάνοια, for the Mind turning from darkness *because of the coming of light*.[1]

---

[1] There are two instances in the New Testament where the idea of Metaméleia, *repentance*, appears in express and designed contrast with the idea of Metanoia, *renewal of mind*.

The first is in Matthew xxi. 32, where the chief priests and the elders are charged not only with their failure to obey at first the proclamation of Renewal of Mind unto Faith in the coming Kingdom and the Christ, by the Baptist, who came to them "in the way of righteousness," but with " not even *repenting*

"*Disastrous Twilight*" in the Revised Version.

The real potency of the new life lay in prospection, not retrospection. It lay in faith, not in fear. It lay in knowledge, not in sorrow. It was an awakening to righteousness, and *therefore* a sinning not. And hence, then, this is the primary word the evangelists and apostles used, whether as initially proclamative or as potentially descriptive of the Christian life; a word profound enough to comprehend, and far-reaching enough to

themselves afterward" (οὐδὲ μετεμελήθητε ὕστερον) when they saw the publicans and harlots "believing" him and entering into the Kingdom of God before them.

The other is in 2 Corinthians vii. 10, where the Corinthians, having been restored to their spiritual senses after a recent demoralization, under the awakening light thrown upon their gross stupefaction by St. Paul, were told by him that now they had come to a Metanoia—a very enthusiasm of righteousness —" a Metanoia *not to be repented of*" (ἀμεταμέλητον).

Here is the only place, by the way, where the revisers felt compelled to change "*repent*" into "regret." The phrase now runs, "a *repentance* which bringeth no *regret*," instead of "a *repentance* not to be *repented* of." St. Paul is also made to "regret," not "*repent*," his severe letter.

How badly mixed were the ideas of the old translators over these, in this striking instance, widely diverging words! And this is all the revisers have done in clarifying their confusion.

The Eclipse of Metánoia by Pœnitentia.

prophesy, the mightiest motive which could energize such a nature as that of man, namely, the personal power of the Son of God; and the mightiest influence which could enter his inmost being to the upbuilding of his character and life, namely, the inspiration of the Spirit of God.

But what the apostolic mind refused to do, even with the legalism of the Old Testament before it, the translating mind, under the influence of that very precedent and of a prevailing fashion of following it, has insisted upon doing. It has insisted upon imposing the translation of the idea of Μεταμέλεια upon the idea of Μετάνοια; and it has undertaken to do what the original writers did not undertake to do—to expand the idea of "*repentance*" (Μεταμέλεια) into the meaning of Μετάνοια. What is more remarkable still, it has undertaken to adapt "*repentance*" to that high expression of Faith unto the Renewal of the spirit of the Mind, even after it has been so thoroughly sophisticated and artificialized under its Romish use, and, we might add, after it has been since so habitually limited by its Protestant interpretation.

VII.

THE POWER OF LATIN PRESCRIPTION.

Now how can we account for all this on the part of a body of men so learned, so judicious, so conscientious, and so courageous as the revisers undoubtedly were? How can we account for their impression that "it was impossible to displace '*repent*,' '*repentance*'"? How can we account for their allowing themselves to be in a position under which the proper disposal of Μετάνοια and Μεταμέλεια, and of the idea of "*repentance*" as supposed to be shared by both, should have "offered great difficulties in translation"? How can we account, also, for the general sentiment of the Christian world which made it so quiet under such a mistranslation that the question was never raised before the revision nor during it—at least not raised enough to make it advisable to take the slightest apparent notice of this gross and dangerous rendering when they passed their microscope over it?

The only answer is a very human and therefore a very humiliating one. It was all owing to the paralyzing power of a long-established precedent—to the impalpable pressure of authority and example. It was all owing to the insidious influence of a Latin tradition, not only as felt in the general Latin texture of English speech, but as it had in this case become embalmed in a body of Latinized doctrine, most ancient and venerable; in a theological spicery strong enough, when diffused in the Jerusalem chamber, to deaden even the sensibility of the alert intelligence which is now awakening to the dawn of a Greek age and a Johannine Christianity. Yes, strange as it may be to think such a thing, it was all owing to the long-armed Vulgate prescription, which had held every previous version of the New Testament in its grip, even from the days of the independent Tyndale, and the power of which was felt even by those who retouched his work at the close of the nineteenth century, even as it was felt by those who had retouched it in the opening of the seventeenth.

What is more remarkable to observe is—by way of showing how persistent and special the descent of this tradition has been—that it appears nowhere else in the version than in this one consecrated line. Whenever Νοῦς by itself, or in any of its other combinations, comes up in the translation, the revisers seem to breathe free, and render it with a full recognition of its noëtic or intellectual element. It is almost an entertaining task to go over all these passages, and to see how fresh this atmosphere is all about them. We had written out the whole of them for insertion here, but this Supplementary Essay is already too long, and we can only give the references. Compare, in all cases, the Revised Version and the suggestive context.

Νοῦς, *mind, understanding.* The revisers, unlike the Authorized Version, have rendered it exclusively so, with the unfortunate exception of not drawing the line between it and φρόνημα, the dispositional idea of mental action. (Luke xxiv. 45; Rom. i. 28, vii. 23,

25, xi. 34, xii. 2, xiv. 5; 1 Cor. i. 10, ii. 16, xiv. 14, 15, 19; Eph. iv. 17, 23; Phil. iv. 7; Col. ii. 18; 2 Thess. ii. 2; 1 Tim. vi. 5; 2 Tim. iii. 8; Tit. i. 15; Rev. xiii. 18, xvii. 9.)

Νέδω, *to see, to perceive, to understand.* (Matt. xv. 17, xvi. 9, 11, xxiv. 15; Mark vii. 18, viii. 17, xiii. 14; John xii. 40; Rom. i. 20; Eph. iii. 4, 20; 1 Tim. i. 17; 2 Tim. ii. 7; Heb. xi. 3.)

Νόημα, *a perception, a thought, a purpose.* (2 Cor. ii. 11, iii. 14, iv. 4, x. 5, xi. 3; Phil. iv. 7.)

Διάνοια, *a thinking through, the mind, the understanding.* (Matt. xxii. 37; Mark xii. 30; Luke i. 51, x. 27; Eph. ii. 3, iv. 18; Col. i. 21; Heb. viii. 10, x. 16; 1 Pet. i. 13; 2 Pet. iii. 1; 1 John v. 20.)

Διανόημα, *thought, purpose.* (Luke xi. 17.)

Ἄνοια, *want of understanding.* (Luke vi. 11; 2 Tim. iii. 9.)

Ἔννοια, *thought, intent, purpose.* (Heb. iv. 12; 1 Pet. iv. 1.)

Ἀνόητος, *unthinking, not understanding.* (Luke xxiv. 25; Rom. i. 14; Gal. iii. 1, 3; 1 Tim. vi. 9; Tit. iii. 3.)

Ἄγνοια, *ignorance.* (Acts iii. 17, xvii. 30; Eph. iv. 18; 1 Pet. i. 14.)

Ἀγνόημα, *ignorance* (involuntary). (Heb. ix. 7, margin.)

Ἐπίνοια, *a thinking upon, thought.* (Acts viii. 22.)

Ὑπόνοια, *a surmise.* (1 Tim. vi. 4.)

Προνοέω, *to foresee, to perceive before.* (Rom. xii. 17; 2 Cor. viii. 21; 1 Tim. v. 8.)

Πρόνοια, *foresight, forethought.* (Acts xxiv. 3; Rom. xiii. 14.)

Ἀγνοέω, *not to perceive, not to know.* (Mark ix. 32; Luke ix. 45; Acts xiii. 27, xvii. 23; Rom. i. 13, ii. 4, vi. 3, vii. 1, x. 3, xi. 25; 1 Cor. xi., xiv. 38; 2 Cor. i. 8, ii. 11, vi. 9; Gal. i. 22; 1 Tim. i. 13; Heb. v. 2; 2 Pet. ii. 12.)

Ὑπονοέω, *to conjecture, to surmise.* (Acts xiii. 25, xxv. 18, xxvii. 27.)

Κατανοέω, *to see or perceive clearly, observe, consider.* (Matt. vii. 3; Luke vi. 41, xii. 24, 27, xx. 23; Acts vii. 31, 32, xi. 6, xxvii. 39; Rom. iv. 19; Heb. iii. 1, x. 24; James i. 23, 24.)

Here are surely instances enough—if not all—limited to close variants of Νοέω and Νοῦς, where their noëtic or perceptive element, the very core of their meaning, is both recognized and rendered by the revisers, often with great spiritual significance.

The Eclipse of Metánoia by Pœnitentia.

But Μετανοέω and Μετάνοια, words from the same mental stem, variants of the same intellectual idea, appear fifty-three times in the Greek Testament, only to disappear in the version! Not a sign, not a suggestion, of their real quality is conveyed to the English reader! They have been kept and set apart to preserve and perpetuate the Latin tradition of "*repent*," "*repentance.*"

The Greek pith has been pushed out of Μετάνοια that it may pipe the *Miserere*!

VIII.

THE TRUE INTERPRETATION.

It would have gone far to soften this situation if the revisers had asked their eminent colleague, who had already done so much in furnishing them with the purest Greek text, to furnish them also with a marginal note which should throw a distinguishing sidelight into their metanoian "*repent*" and "*repentance.*" If they had, it would probably have been this: "*A general Change of Mind, which becomes in its fullest development an intellectual and moral Regeneration.*" And if they had, these old Latin words, so palpably inadequate and incongruous, would have been on the way to be "displaced," both unceremoniously and soon.

But as the margin has been left without this illustration, the only alternative now would seem to be the very unsatisfactory one which is intimated in Bishop Westcott's personal note to us:

"The preacher and the scholar must transfigure '*repentance*,' even as *fides* and *gratia* have been transfigured. In this work your essay will, I trust, be of eminent service."

Which can only mean that, the revisers having failed to do it, or to do anything about it, the task of making the best of an inadequate and misleading translation is now thrown upon the pulpit and the commentators.

This is not a pleasant fact to face: that the original Scriptures should, in any essential part or in any vital word, be so incommunicable to the people, that the people must be dependent upon their teachers not only for exposition, but for revelation itself. Such, we take it, is not the true idea of a version, and one may well be impatient if the cause for it should not reside in the original, but in some conventionalism of habit or taste or theory or principle on the part of the translators, which has abridged the capacity of our own language. And one may be sure that if darkness does still rest on any por-

The True Interpretation.

tion of our version the fault lies in a hesitation to employ the full freedom of the English tongue. But we do not say, in saying this, that any darkness, or shadow of darkness, still lingers over the work of the revisers because of their unwillingness to remove it through any such cause, or that they were conscious of any such cause, even in regard to this rendering of Μετάνοια.

Most especially do we personally feel this when we have the great scholar and preacher in mind who sat so high in the counsels of the revisers, and upon whose endorsement of our exposition of the Greek word we set so high a value. We have ventured to differ with him only on a question of judgment, wherein he may be wise and we unwise. He would not disturb a rendering around which for ages many venerable associations have gathered, and the removal of which would disarrange many doctrinal conceptions. As he looks upon it, to "displace" it would be to displace a corner-stone; and though he is ready to admit that it was "originally inadequate," yet he evidently thinks less harm would result if it were quietly and

The Eclipse of Metánoia by Pœnitentia.

gradually changed for another, which, though retaining the name, would be the genuine stone. Such a substitution, he thinks, would become practicable in the progress of public sentiment, or, as he calls it, "Christian use." Doubtless there are many who would agree with him in this method of meeting the enormous difficulty of repairing a very serious error which has so many ages for its sanction and a remote antiquity for its origin.

Our own belief in the utter impracticability of this way of dealing with it we have now tried to express in the best way we could. We would make the change at once in the text of the translation. We would remove the idea and the words *"repent," "repentance"* from every part of the New Testament except where they represent the idea of Μεταμέλεια; and we would have it so, that no sermon or treatise should employ the expressions except in the sense of "sorrow" or "regret." And we would do this *now* in the interest of truth, in the interest of genuine Christianity, in the interest of an age which does not fear to face a fact, whatever be the consequences.

As we have said before, so we say again:

The True Interpretation.

we do not believe in the process of "transfiguration," when it is to be attempted upon a word of such a character, and containing in itself such a latent dogmatic force, as "*repentance.*" The only safety is in letting it, dogmatically, alone, in dropping it, dogmatically, out, and in retaining it only in its popular and strictly Scriptural sense—a regret for something that is past, and a regret that, in a matter of wrong-doing, may deepen into a "godly sorrow"; and this "regret" we would always call "*repent.*" All this we say because we believe that, so long as the word is used for Μετάνοια, the characteristic key-note of Christianity will give not only an uncertain, but a radically reversing, as well as a misleading, sound: the world will lose the original and innermost, the initial and guiding principle of the religion of Jesus Christ.

In regard to the instances mentioned by Bishop Westcott of the successful transfigurement of "faith" and "grace," despite their Latin perversion, it seems to us that they are hardly a parallel. Only theologians are familiar with any ancient association of those words which would despoil them now of their depth and beauty. They have become thoroughly English. They have no harsh historic physiognomy to soften away. In neither of them are we obliged to lift off a Latin cowl in order to bare a Greek brow. The deep heart of their Greek originals is easily to be seen in the countenance of both.

And now we must add, in view of the kind suggestion that in the work of "transfiguring" *repentance*, our essay may be "of eminent service," that we could look upon it with but little satisfaction if we thought that, after all, we had only succeeded in expounding the force of "*repentance*" in a way that reconciled the preacher and scholar the more to the old rendering, and had only helped, therefore, to confirm the esoteric position in which the word at present stands, namely, a position under which those who are learned may have one consciousness in reading it in the New Testament, and those who are not learned, another.

In conclusion let us express again the immense satisfaction that we have taken in the remarkable definition of Μετάνοια by this distinguished scholar and theologian, an eminent authority in Greek and a master in English, of world-wide fame. We place it with pride beside those of De Quincey and Matthew Arnold, as the expression of a spiritual perception and experience which combines the force of both:

Μετάνοια *describes Characteristically in the Language of the New Testament, a General Change of Mind, which Becomes in its Fullest Development an Intellectual and Moral Regeneration.*"

ASSENTING WITNESSES.

THE following letters—extracts for the most part—were written without a thought of publication. They are simple, unstudied, and spontaneous expressions of interest in the subject. They all refer, of course, to the first essay, and have been selected out of a large number (received from time to time since its publication) because of their suggestiveness, the weightiness of their indorsement, and their contributary character, in one way or another, to the substance of the essay itself.

It was at first designed, when the reissue of the essay was thought of, to make each of them the base of a sort of excursus, of greater or less length—the whole group of which, taken together, leading out into various aspects of the subject, and developing its Scriptural and theological, as well as its philosophical and practical relations and bearings.

The material for all this has, however, been laid aside, under an exigency which has made it undesirable for the present reprint, and the plan has only been carried out in the instance of the first of the letters. (See the second essay.) There were several others of striking character which have consequently been omitted, as the field of thought they opened required especial consideration in order to elicit their true value.

I.

From the Rt. Rev. Brooke Foss Westcott, D.D., D.C.L., Bishop of Durham, late Canon of Westminster, and Regius Professor of Divinity, Cambridge; a member of the English New Testament Company of the Revisers:

"There was a reference to your essay in a paper on the Revised Version, in the 'Expositor.' I have not a copy of the magazine at hand, but I think it was in the paper which appeared in August.

"I intended to say that you had brought out with singular power and truth the meaning of Μετάνοια, while I could not see that the translation could be modified.

"The preacher and the scholar must transfigure

'*repentance*,' even as '*fides*' and '*gratia*' have been transfigured. In this work your essay will, I trust, be of eminent service.
"B. F. WESTCOTT."

II.

From the Rev. Alexander Roberts, D.D., Professor of Humanity in the University of St. Andrews, a member of the English New Testament Company of the Revisers, and author of the "Companion to the Revised Version of the New Testament, Explaining the Reasons for the Changes Made in the Authorized Version." This handbook accompanied the issue of the Revised Version in May, 1881.

"I have read with much interest your thoughtful and valuable paper on 'Metánoia.'

"The expression '*repentance*,' though plainly inadequate as a translation of it, has so rooted itself in our language that it seems almost impossible to get rid of it.

"However, we have manifestly entered on an epoch of revision, and I trust you will bring your suggestions under the notice of anybody that may be appointed, in order, if possible, to provide an English version of the New Testament which may meet with general acceptance. . . .
"ALEXANDER ROBERTS."

Assenting Witnesses.

From the same at a later date.

"I hope some effectual means will be found for bringing your original and striking exposition of Μετάνοια under the notice of scholars in this country.

"I shall see that it is submitted to those of my colleagues who are likely to take an interest in the subject.

"ALEXANDER ROBERTS."

III.

From the Rev. Howard Crosby, D.D., LL.D., ex-Chancellor of the University of New York, a member of the American New Testament Company of the Revisers.

"I think you are quite right.

"I have always taught that the Metanoia of the Gospel was not a sorrow for sin, but an *abandonment* of sin.

"Its classical meaning is 'a change of view and plan,' as in that intensely interesting part of Thucydides where the Athenians order the destruction of the Mityleneans, and then on the next day *repent.* There is not a particle of mourning over sin in that.

"Of course when one *repents* (μετανοεῖ) from sin there will be a godly sorrow, but *this is not in the word.*

"The Metanoia of the Jews was, as you say, a change of view (and plan) from the *pronoian* condition. Those at Pentecost thus *repented*, although, doubtless, the majority of them were truly godly men before.

"HOWARD CROSBY."

IV.

From the Rev. Philip Schaff, D.D., LL.D., Professor of Sacred Literature in the Union Theological Seminary, New York, President of the American Revision Committee, author of "A Companion to the Greek Testament and the English Version," etc.

" Many thanks to you for your able, excellent, and truthful article on the meaning of Μετάνοια, which has my cordial approval.

" Conservatism prevented a change, and the difficulty of substituting a precise equivalent in one word.

"PHILIP SCHAFF."

V.

From the Very Rev. E. H. Plumptre, D.D., Dean of Wells, a member of the English Old Testament Company.

" Pray accept my best thanks for your very suggestive paper.

" I quite agree with you as to the inadequacy of the accepted rendering of Μετάνοια, but I do not see any way to a better one as yet.

"'Resipiscence' was an attempt, but it proved abortive.

"'Change of mind' or 'principles' or 'heart' is cumbrous, and leaves the nature of the change undefined.

"E. H. PLUMPTRE."

VI.

From the Rev. Edward White, author of "Life in Christ," "Mystery of Growth," etc.

"LONDON, 1892.

"Some one has sent me a copy of your tract on Μετάνοια, but the sender has remained anonymous.

"I thank the sender anyway—and the author.

"The argument has been familiar to me for fifty years, and I have always regarded it as unanswerable and most important.

"I learned its nature and irresistible force in early life by reading Dr. George Campbell's 'Preliminary Dissertations on the Gospels' (Principal of Marischal College, Aberdeen, Scotland) (Preliminary Dissertation No. VI.), where a very precise, full, and decisive argument, both critical and spiritual, fixes the *practical* sense of Μετάνοια as you have done.

"There are some valuable points brought out by Principal Campbell, which I think will interest you, in *addition* to your own.

"No doubt Dr. Campbell's 'Dissertations' are to be seen in some of your theological libraries. It is a golden book, almost forgotten in the crowd of modern works.

"I trust that your endeavors will result in some wholesome teaching on the subject of the true Μετά-νοια in the United States.

"EDWARD WHITE,
"*Author of 'Life in Christ.'*"

VII.

From the Rev. Alexander V. G. Allen, D.D., Professor in the Episcopal Theological School, Cambridge, Mass., author of "The Continuity of Christian Thought: A Study of Modern Theology in the Light of its History," etc.

1884.

"I have read your paper on the 'Metanoia,' and am greatly delighted with it.

"The thought of it goes deep down into the very heart of the Christian revelation, and when the full meaning of your position is taken, one can see that it is the hinge upon which a truer and larger conception of Christianity must turn.

"It seems to me that we have been thinking in the same direction.

"You have brought out the importance of the fact that the new revelation found its first expression in the Greek language; and to that language we must turn, if we are to get the fresh original idea in the mind of its first disciples.

Assenting Witnesses.

"When the New Testament was translated in Latin there came a profound misapprehension of its central positions. 'Metanoia' is one word. So another is 'grace,' and another is 'justification'—words which fall far short as Latin equivalents for the original Greek.

"I have begun later than you in taking up the same issue; i.e., with the Greek fathers as the best interpreters of Christianity, because they were under the influence of that culture which was divinely appointed to create a language for the new order.

"The Latins disowned philosophy and human culture. They were inclined, like true Romans, to put all the mischief in the will; heresy was a vicious wilfulness; and the trouble with the will was a weakness or impotence toward right, which had been inherited from Adam. This vicious direction of the will could only be overcome by omnipotent power bearing down all finite opposition, and this power which acts upon the will (grace) is conveyed through outward channels.

"That was the substance of Augustinianism and of Latin Christianity. It disowned the intellect as having any vital connection with the regenerated life.

"With the Greeks it was knowledge, which must overcome the ignorance of man; but this knowledge carried with it the whole nature, as you have shown.

"The essay is a beautiful, clear, and original statement of a great issue.

"A. V. G. ALLEN."

VIII.

From the Rev. J. F. Garrison, D.D., Professor in the Protestant Episcopal Divinity School, Philadelphia.

"I hope the old saw, 'Better late than never,' will hold good in my acknowledgment, at this late day, of the interest and value of your article on 'Metanoia.'

"I have had my pen in hand many times to do it, but there was so much I wished to say about it that each time I waited for a 'more convenient season,' until now, in utter despair of finding leisure for this, I cannot refrain longer to tell you how profoundly important I feel the points you make to be.

"I have been so deeply impressed with them for twenty years that I scarcely or never use the word '*repent*' in any of its Bible references without pausing to reiterate the true meaning of the mental and spiritual process implied in the Metanoia.

"And I am sure that many of our most disastrous failures in commending Christianity to unbelieving minds—especially minds of a manly character—have their cause just here.

"You have thought so much on the bearings of the idea that I need not tell you how or why.

"What I wanted, however, especially to enlarge upon were certain of the collateral relations of the word, and its psychological connections, which I have felt to be at the same time confirmations of your views and expressions of its great meaning.

Assenting Witnesses.

"I can only hint at them, as it has been my inability to write more fully which has let me hitherto, and I doubt not but they have occurred to you.

"1. One of these is the analogy of the use of the word in the Greek of the LXX., wherein very often the passages rendered '*repent*,' etc., in the Authorized Version are given in the Septuagint by Μετανοεῖν, etc., with a most decided advantage to the clearness, consistency, and satisfactoriness of the passage.

"2. The remarkable significance of the word Νοῦς and all its derivatives in the philosophic language of that age, as we learn this from the Greek, especially the Alexandrian, writers. And I more and more believe that the language of the writers of the New Testament had much in common with this.

"I cannot pause even to outline my grounds for this, but they are so strong to my mind that if I were in the middle instead of near the end of my mental life-work I would make it the theme of an elaborate volume.

"Now, in all the prevalent thought of that time, 'thought' (νοῦς as its reality) and 'being' were only *two sides of one and the same essence.* With them the Real was not, as with us, the Material, but the Noëtic. What on the side of consciousness and actual verity was νοεῖν (thought), on its side of real existence was εἶναι. To think was 'to be,' and 'to be' was essentially thought. The Spiritual was the Real, and the only Real was the Spiritual.

"(And herein lies the essence of the endless discussion on the Real Presence. The hard-headed Latin could never see that anything was Real that he could not represent as *quasi* Material.)

"Now, with this conception of νοεῖν, go back to Metanoia, and we have the complete expression and magnificent sweep of the full thought. In changing the νοεῖν of the man he has become changed in the very essence of his εἶναι; 'all things have become new.'

"I need not evolve the thought further. It lies at the foundation of the whole Alexandrian, or rather of the whole philosophic, thought of that age, and in Plotinus is developed to the dialectic system with which he hoped to rival Christianity, but which, by its one-sided character, made it only a sublime dream for the few instead of a divine life for the many.

"3. As a relique of my old medical life. Insanity is not, as I think, an error of reasoning. Who reasons so inexorably as an insane man? 'I am—my mind (νοῦς) tells me—a king. Therefore I can and will do as a king.' And all he does follows on strictest reasoning from his νοεῖν. Change his essential accepted thought—self—and at once he 'is' a different man. As he 'thought' in his essential self, so he 'was.' His Μετάνοια at once changes his entire 'being.'

"I have often presented this as a terrible analogy to the condition of man as a sinner. By nature he accepts as the essential fact of his being, in his thought, 'this world, self, sin, as all-real, all-sufficient.' Christ comes and says, 'Your whole being and thought are wrong. Μετανοεῖτε: let your whole being and thought turn from this. It is a lie, and you and your life, based on it, a delusion; for there is a kingdom of the heavens which is THE truth,' etc.

"Here, again, I only put a finger-mark; but the meaning of the whole is, I thank you very heartily for your admirable and needed paper.

"J. F. GARRISON."

IX.

From the Rev. Elisha Mulford, LL.D., author of "The Republic of God," "The Nation," etc.

"The essay has very great value. It gives the view of the term which I have long held.

"This is the one term which connects most clearly the errand of St. John the Baptist with the message of the Gospel.

"It has more direct and full significance than those to which I note a reference in Hausrath's 'Times of Jesus,' tr., ii., p. 120.

"The grammarians have always underrated De Quincey.

"ELISHA MULFORD."

X.

From the Rev. Edward T. Bartlett, D.D., Dean of the Protestant Episcopal Divinity School, Philadelphia.

"I am greatly indebted to you for your essay on the great New Testament word.

"At a glance I saw much of its value, but now that I have carefully studied it I think it wonderful and of permanent worth for its scholarship and its true fervor, the like of which in combination I do not remember to have ever seen.

"The ability with which you present your great subject and marshal your grand argument seems to me absolutely perfect, and should make this essay one that will be the standard monograph on the subject.

"If I could wish for any addition to your treatment of the subject it would be as to the fuller development of the truth that the change of the mind itself may precede and lead to a change of circumstance—the truth which Dr. Bushnell, e.g., brings out in those two tremendous sermons, 'The Bad Consciousness Taken Away,' and 'The Bad Mind Makes a Bad Element,' in his 'Christ and His Salvation.'

"I did not mean to say this, but will venture to let it go, almost sure, though, that upon further study of your essay, which I intend to make, I shall find that you have given that truth all the emphasis it needed, and that I have been mistaken.

"Again I thank you for the keen pleasure you have afforded me in your beautiful paper.

"EDWARD T. BARTLETT."

From the same at a recent date.

"I am glad to know that a new edition of 'Metanoia' is to be given us. Strong evidence that the

Assenting Witnesses.

view you take has permanently impressed thoughtful men as one of deep value and importance has been meeting me ever and anon for years.

"My suggestion when I saw you in Boston was to this effect: that you should go straight through the New Testament and carefully work out each passage where the word occurs, or its cognates, and show how the real meaning can be put into good smooth English expression. Some work I am doing has led me to study the matter closely and to try to do this very thing. . . . It would not take much space. An appendix of a few pages would surely be enough. Such a thing would be most timely. I beg you to do it.

"EDWARD T. BARTLETT."

XI.

From the Rev. Benjamin Franklin, D.D., author of "'The Creed and Modern Thought."

"May I venture to express the great pleasure and sense of mental benefit with which I have read your article in the July number of the 'American Church Review'?

"You have undoubtedly made an intrinsic contribution to the theology of the age, and given an illustration of what many have thought and some have said, viz., that 'Catholic theology' is as much alive in this age, and as well adapted to current thought, as it ever has been.

"The article, while learned and able, of course,

Assenting Witnesses.

is abreast of the age, and takes that humanly sympathetic yet distinctively Christian stand which primitive Christianity occupied.

"As a work emanating from the theological school to which you are popularly assigned, it of course looks at the truth from its own point of view.

"It does so admirably, however, and will, I hope, so permeate the mind of preachers that the Gospel, on its human side, may be better preached, and men induced to recognize and develop, in mind and heart, their original godlikeness.

"B. FRANKLIN."

XII.

From the Rt. Rev. Phillips Brooks, D.D., Bishop of Massachusetts.

"It is full of inspiration.

"It makes one think of Christian faith as positive and constructive, and not merely destructive and remedial.

"It makes the work of Christ seem worthy of Christ.

"PHILLIPS BROOKS."

www.ingramcontent.com/pod-product-compliance
Lightning Source LLC
Chambersburg PA
CBHW020245170426
43202CB00008B/227